THINK AND DRAW LIKE AN ARTIST

A Creative Guide to Mastering Anatomy and Form

Ait elhaj

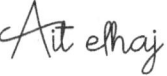

LEARNING TO DRAW IS A REWARDING
JOURNEY THAT COMBINES PRACTICE,
OBSERVATION, AND A BIT OF PATIENCE.
HERE'S A GUIDE TO HELP YOU GET STARTED
AND DEVELOP YOUR SKILLS :

1. Start with the basics: shapes and lines

Use simple shapes: Drawing is mainly about finding objects and breaking them down into basic shapes (circles, squares, rectangles). Draw these shapes habitually to get comfortable with line control.

Work on the use of lines and tension: Practice drawing light dark lines, as well as straight lines and curves. This will improve your hand control.

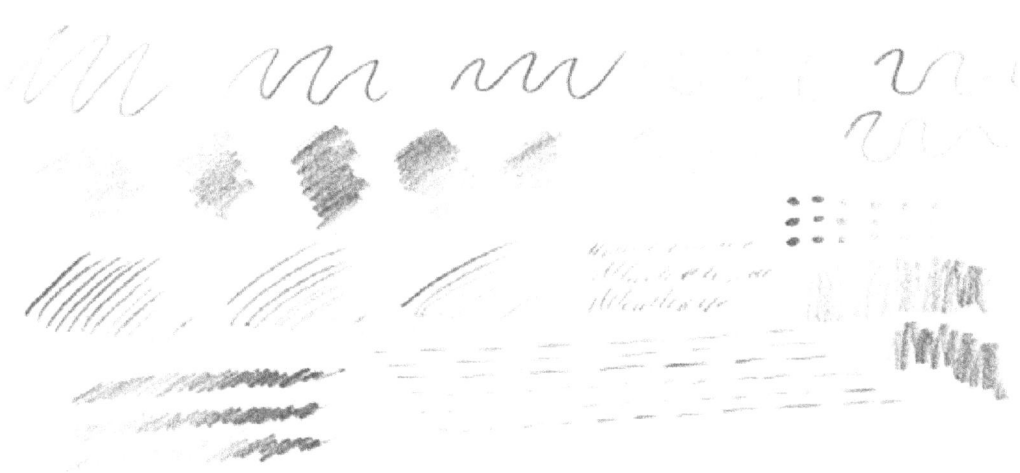

2. Learn to observe

Use Observation: Just take the time to observe and notice details. Pay close attention to shapes, shadows, angles, how the parts interact.

Contour Drawing: Try to draw an object without looking at your paper. This forces you to focus on the shape and contours of the object, creating hand-eye coordination.

3. Start with simple headlines

Stay alive: Start with basic surroundings like a bowl, fruit, or a book. These are great for proportion, shading and applying perspective.

Draw from reference: Use pictures or diagrams to practice. Websites like Pinterest, Unsplash, or photography apps in particular can make good reference images.

4. Use coherent reasoning and perspective

Unit: Learn the basic similarities between objects and people. For example, the human body is usually about 7-8 heads tall, with the eyes halfway up.
Perspective: Understanding perspective (1-point, 2-point, and 3-point) will help draw objects in 3D space. Start by practicing cube and box perspectives to see what things look like from different angles.

5. Apply Shading and Textures

Learn basic shading: Use shading techniques to create depth, such as hatching, cross-hatching and blending. Use shading to show where the light hits and the shadows fall.
Use texture: Try to pull in different textures like wood, metal, or fabric. This will help add realism to your photos.

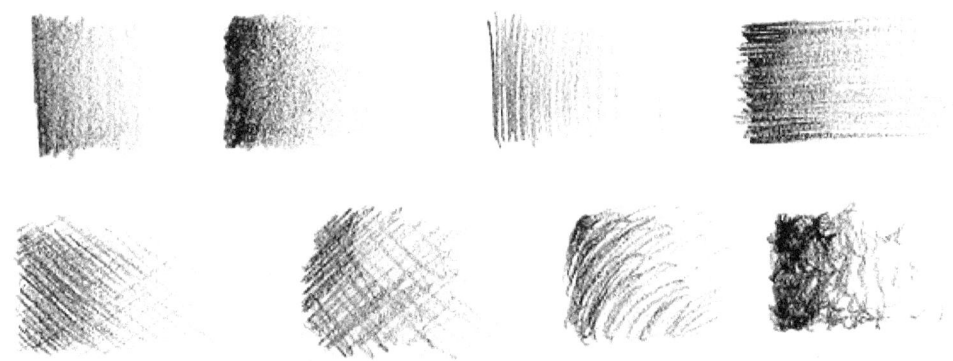

6. Learn about anatomy (for drawing) .

Basic anatomy: If you love drawing people or animals, start with basic anatomy. Understanding how muscles and bones work makes your drawings look more realistic.
Drawing Signs: Learn to quickly visualize people or animals engaged in situations. This will help you capture movement and symmetry without focusing too much on details.

7. Use Tutorials and Books

Follow the step-by-step tutorial: There are plenty of online tutorials on YouTube, websites, and social media that break down the drawing process. Following it can be very helpful for beginners.
Study drawing books: Books like "Drawing on the Right Side of the Brain" by Betty Edwards or "Figure Drawing for All It's Worth" by Andrew Loomis provide excellent guidance for beginners.

8. Experiment with different media

Try pencils, charcoal, pens, or digital tools: Different tools can help you discover new techniques. It is often recommended to start with a pencil as this makes it easier to correct.

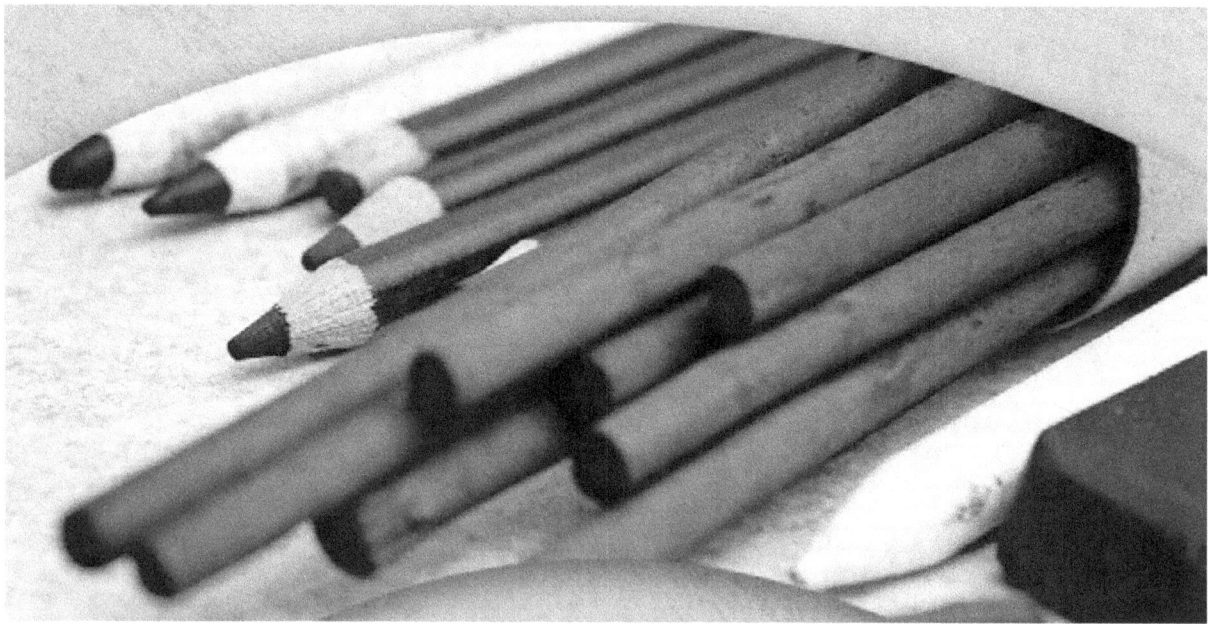

9. Make a sketchbook and draw daily

Consistency is key. Try to draw something every day, even if it's a small doodle. This helps with muscle memory and improves your skills over time.
Use a sketchbook and keep all your exercises in one place. It's a great way to track your progress.

10. Get feedback and reflect on your work

Ask for constructive feedback: Show your work to others, join online art communities, or take drawing classes to get feedback on your progress.
Reflect and adjust: Look back at your career to see where you improved and where you could focus more effort.

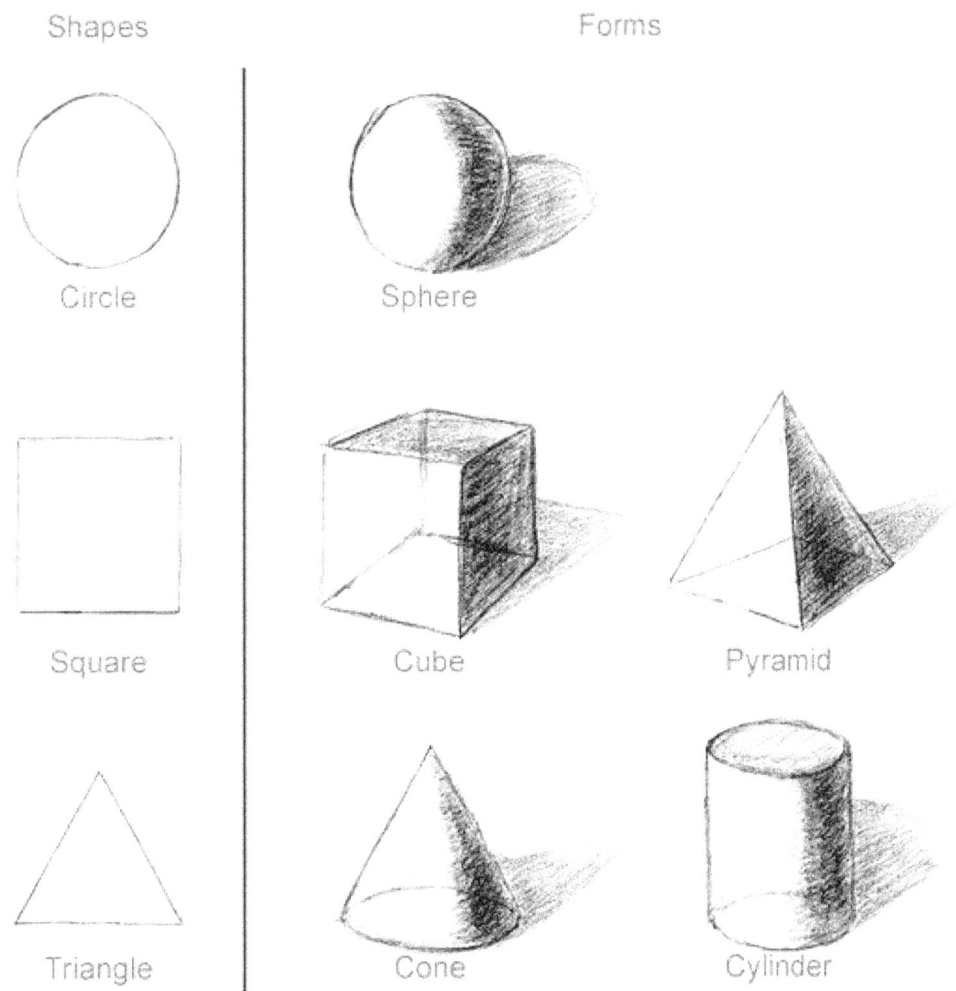

Remember :

- Drawing is a skill that anyone can learn with practice. Don't worry about "talent" improvement comes with patience, curiosity, and time.

- Enjoy the process and give yourself room to experiment, make mistakes, and try again.

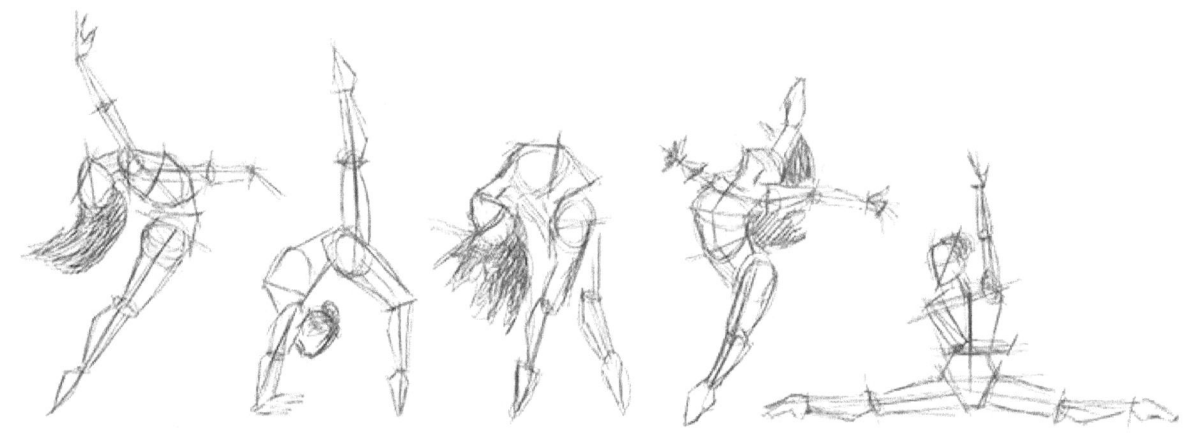

Good luck, and happy drawing!

You can find it hard , but it is easier if you break it down into simple steps. Here's a basic guide:

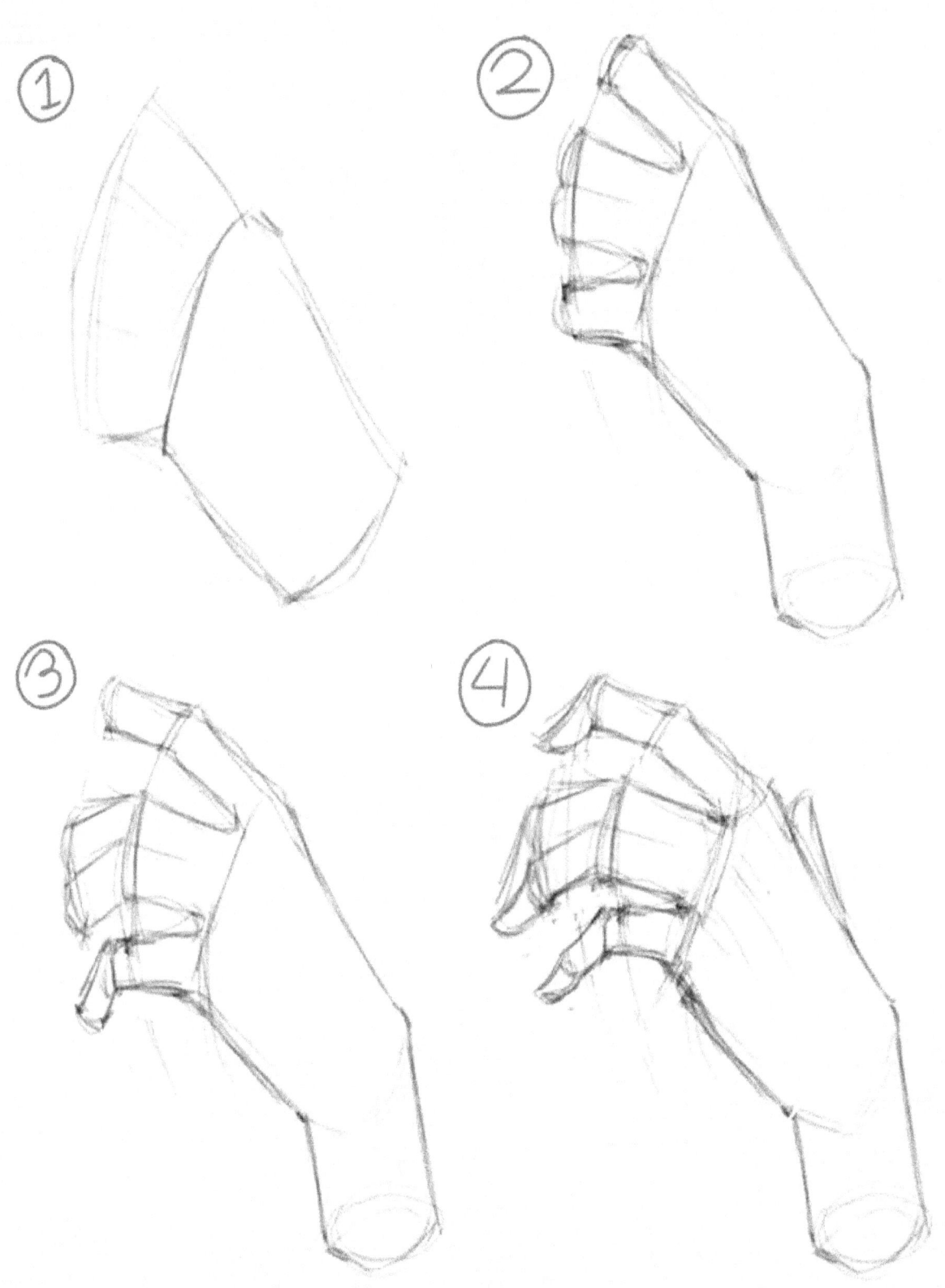

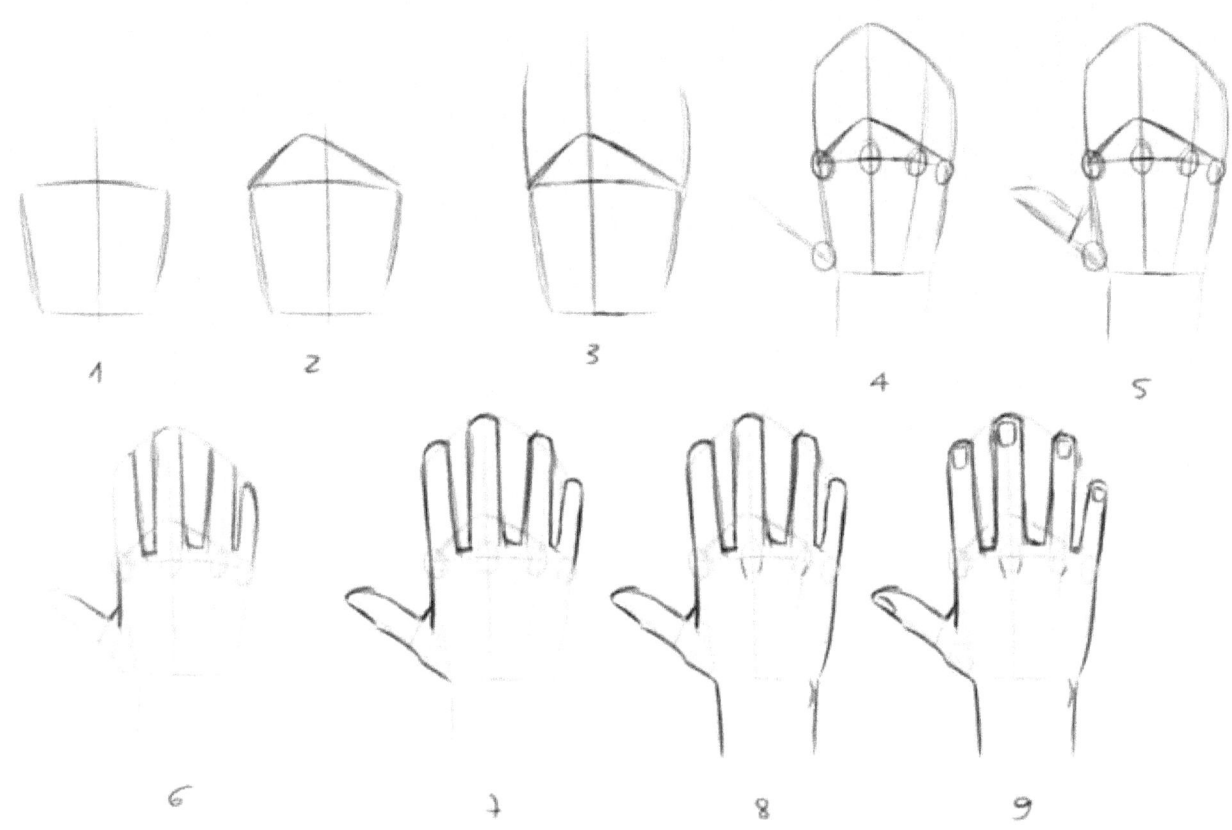

- Tart with the Palm and Wrist

Create an oval or rectangle to represent the hand's main bulk (the palm).
Draw two lines coming down from the oval/rectangle to build the wrist.
Add the Fingers, Guidelines for each finger that extend up from the top of
the palm. It can start with simple lines (initially) lining where each finger is
located.

Part each of the guidelines into three parts for the joints. While the
thumb consists of two segments, fingers generally contain three.

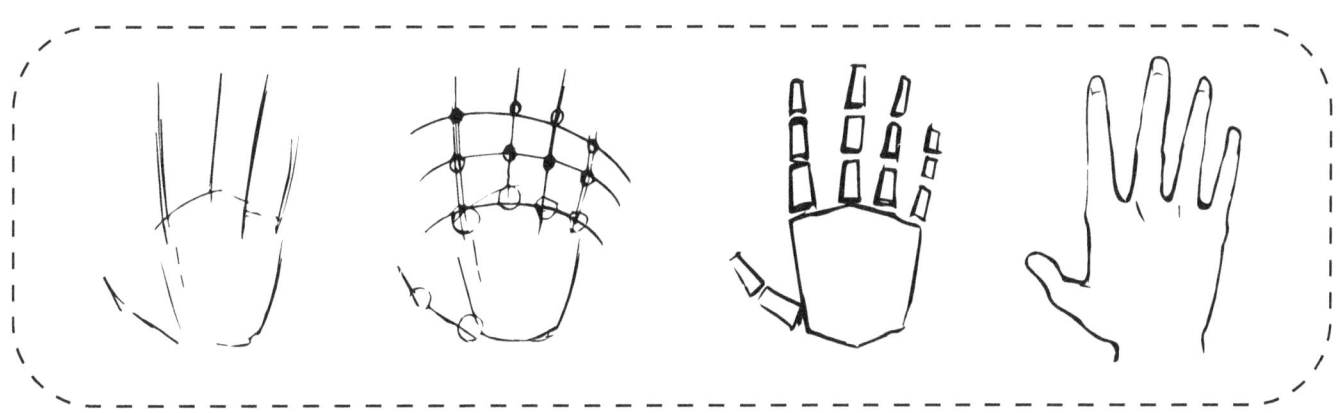

Exercise every finger

Using the guidelines, trace the outline of each finger, tapering slightly towards the edges. Remember that the fingers are not perfectly straight; have slight curves. The middle finger is usually the longest, followed by the index and ring fingers, then the little finger.

Draw the thumb

Place your thumb at an angle to your palm, usually about 45 degrees. It starts lower in the hand and has a more flexible shape.
Draw two segments for the thumb, with the tip slightly rounded.

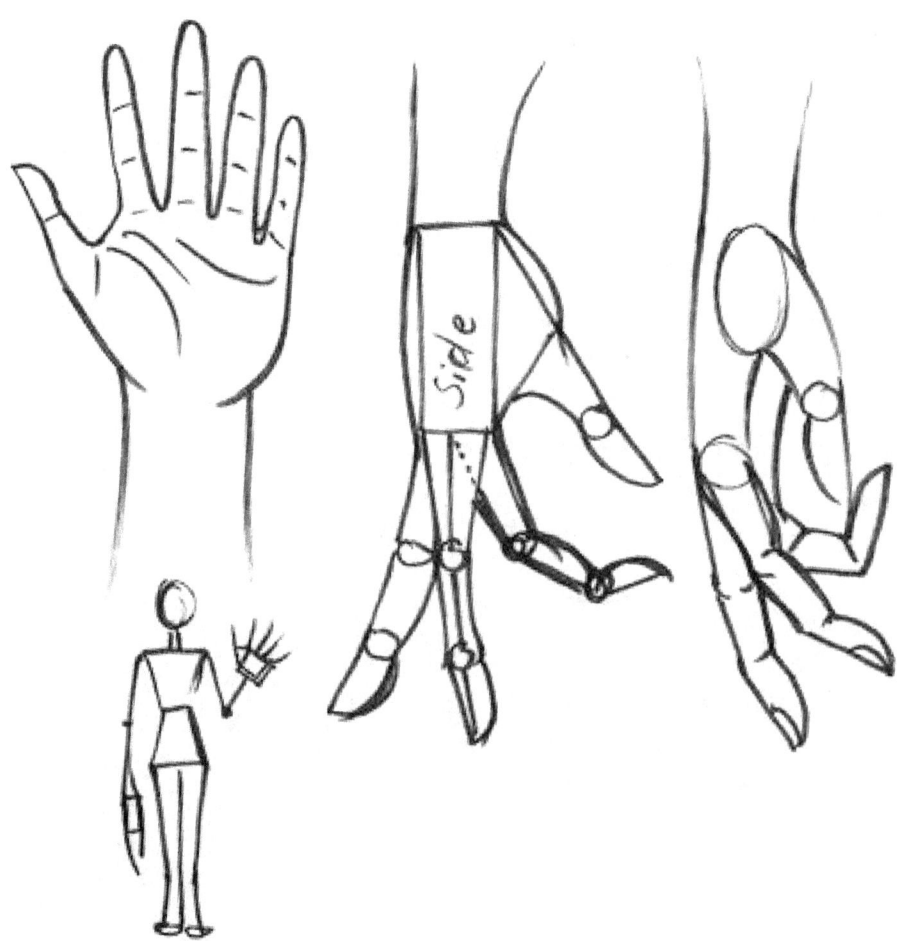

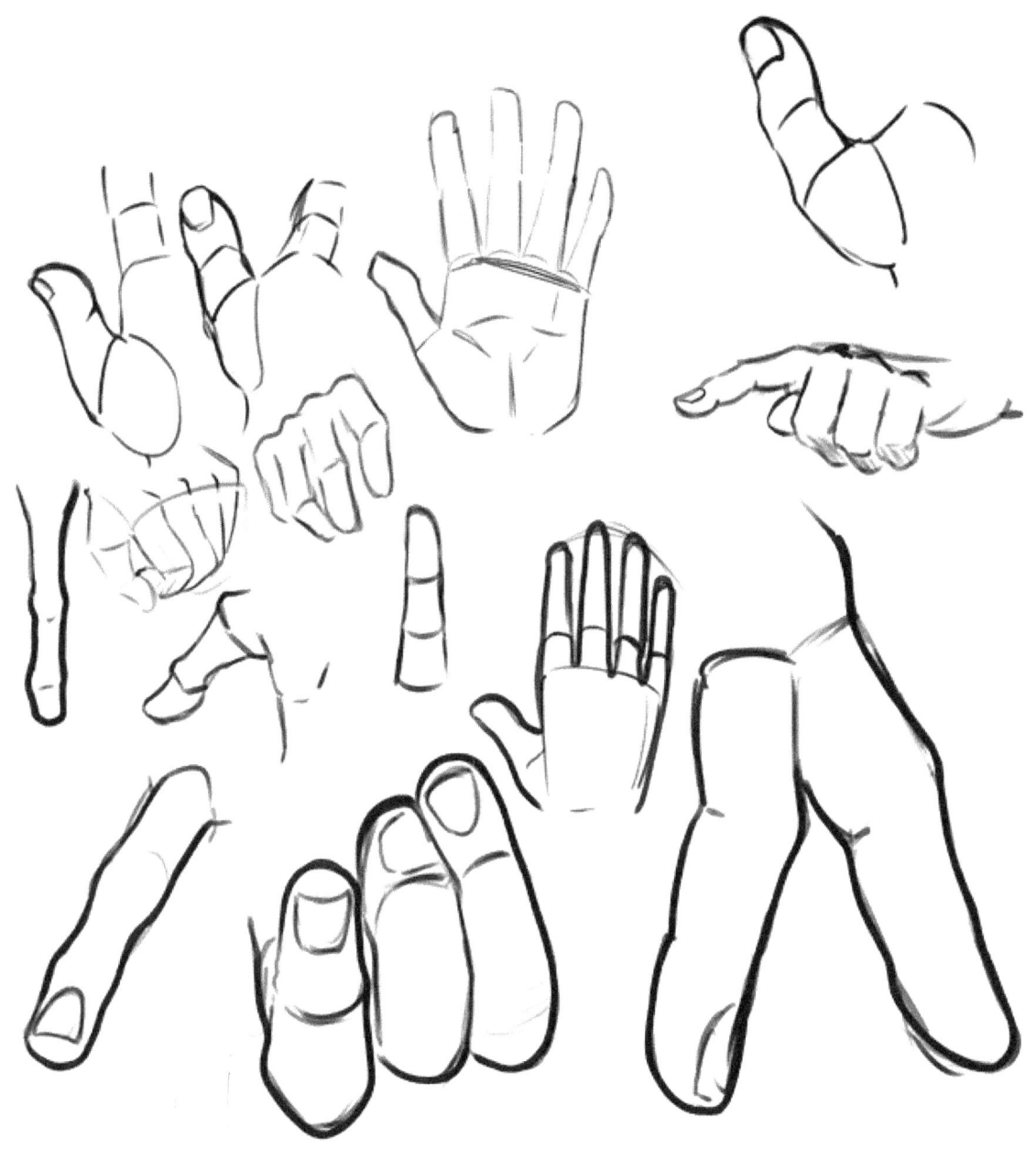

Add Joints and Knuckles

Lightly sketch the knuckles and joints on each finger. Knuckles are typically more pronounced on the back of the hand.

Refine the Outline and Erase Guidelines

Smooth out the lines to create a natural hand shape, erasing unnecessary guidelines.
Add details like wrinkles and folds where fingers bend and around the palm.

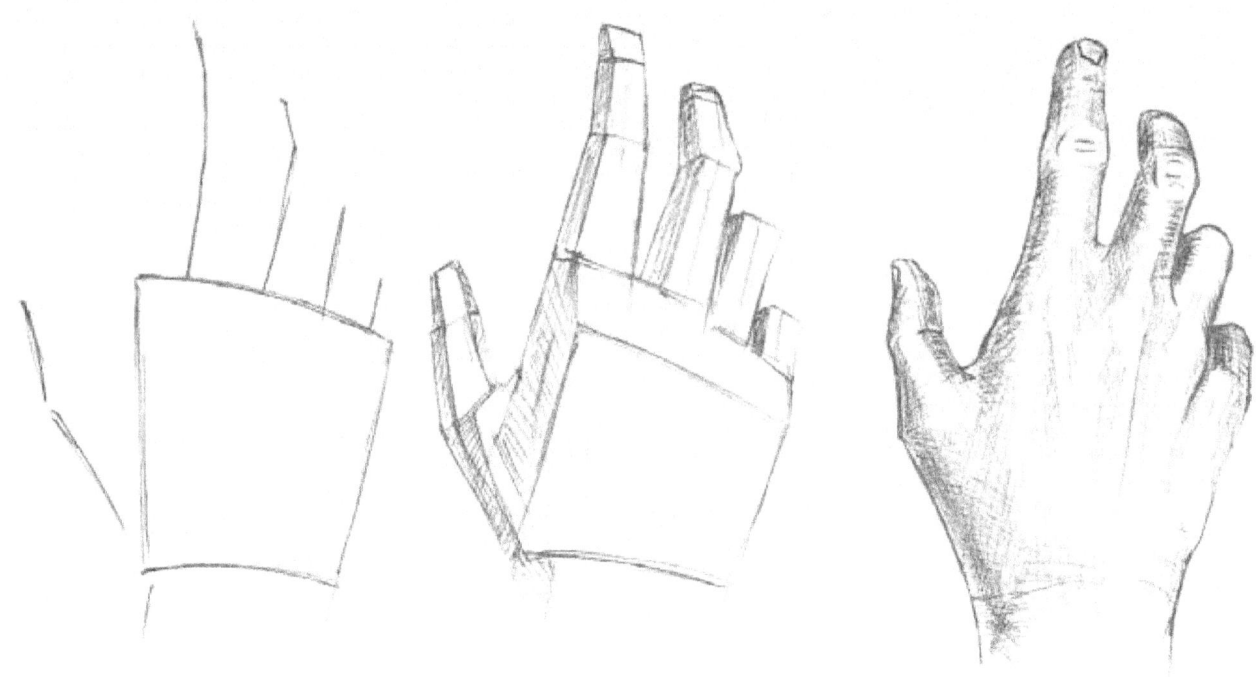

Shade for Depth

To make the hand look realistic, add shading to indicate light and shadow, especially around the creases, knuckles, and under the fingers.

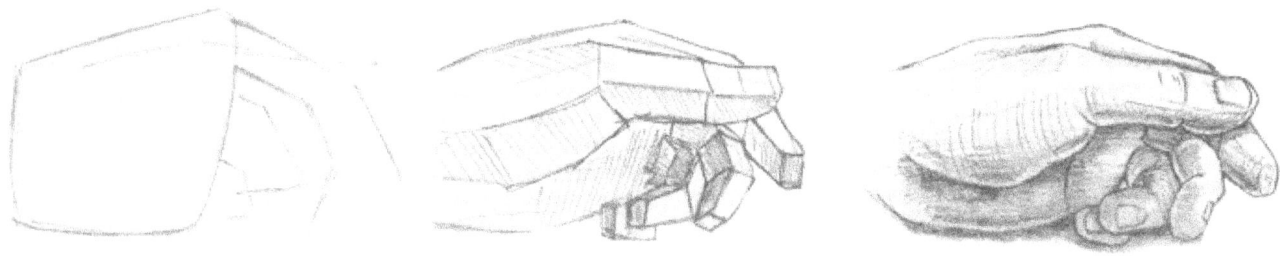

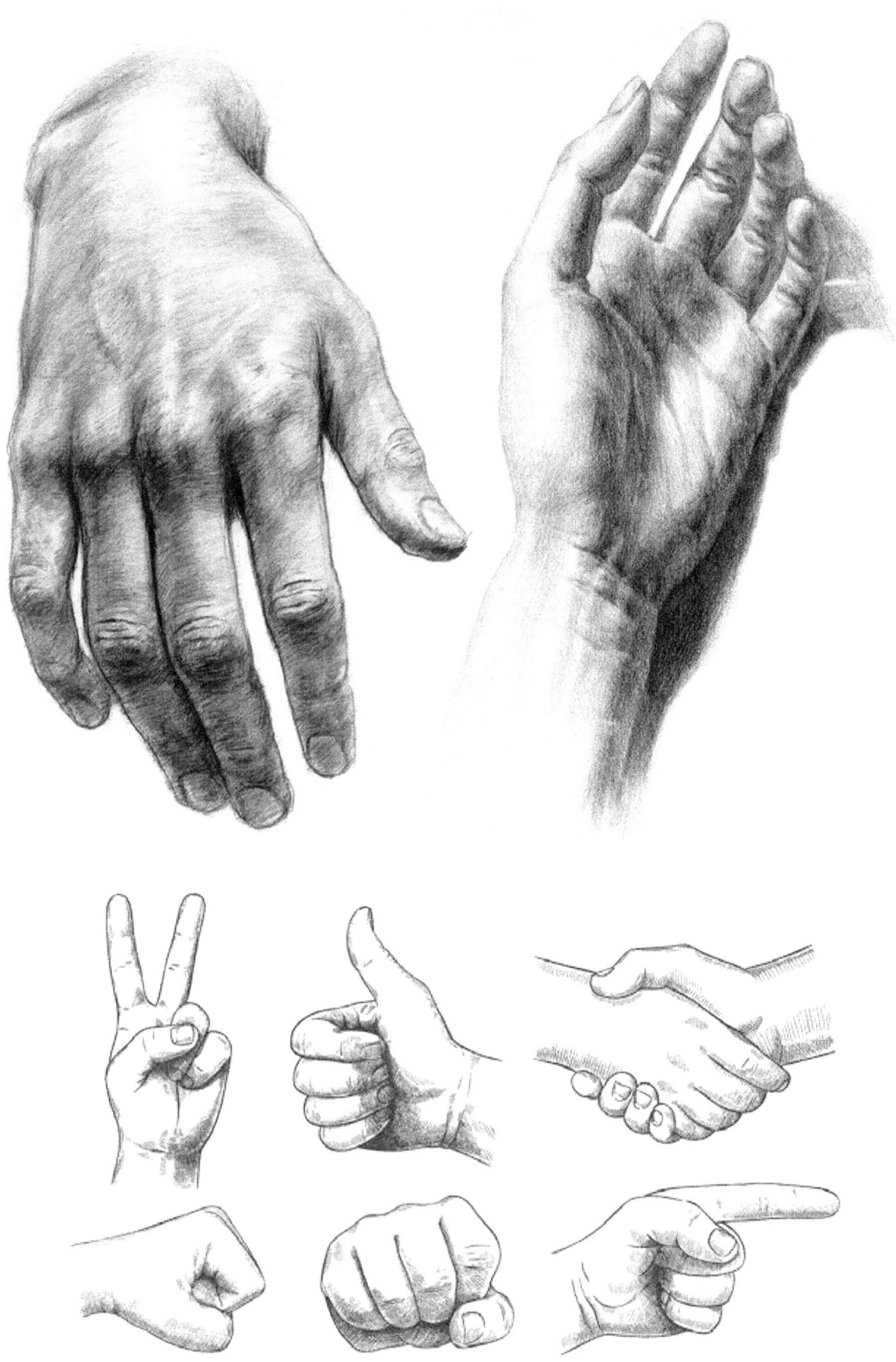

Drawing legs can be simplified by breaking down the main shapes and proportions.
Here's a step-by-step guide to help you get started:

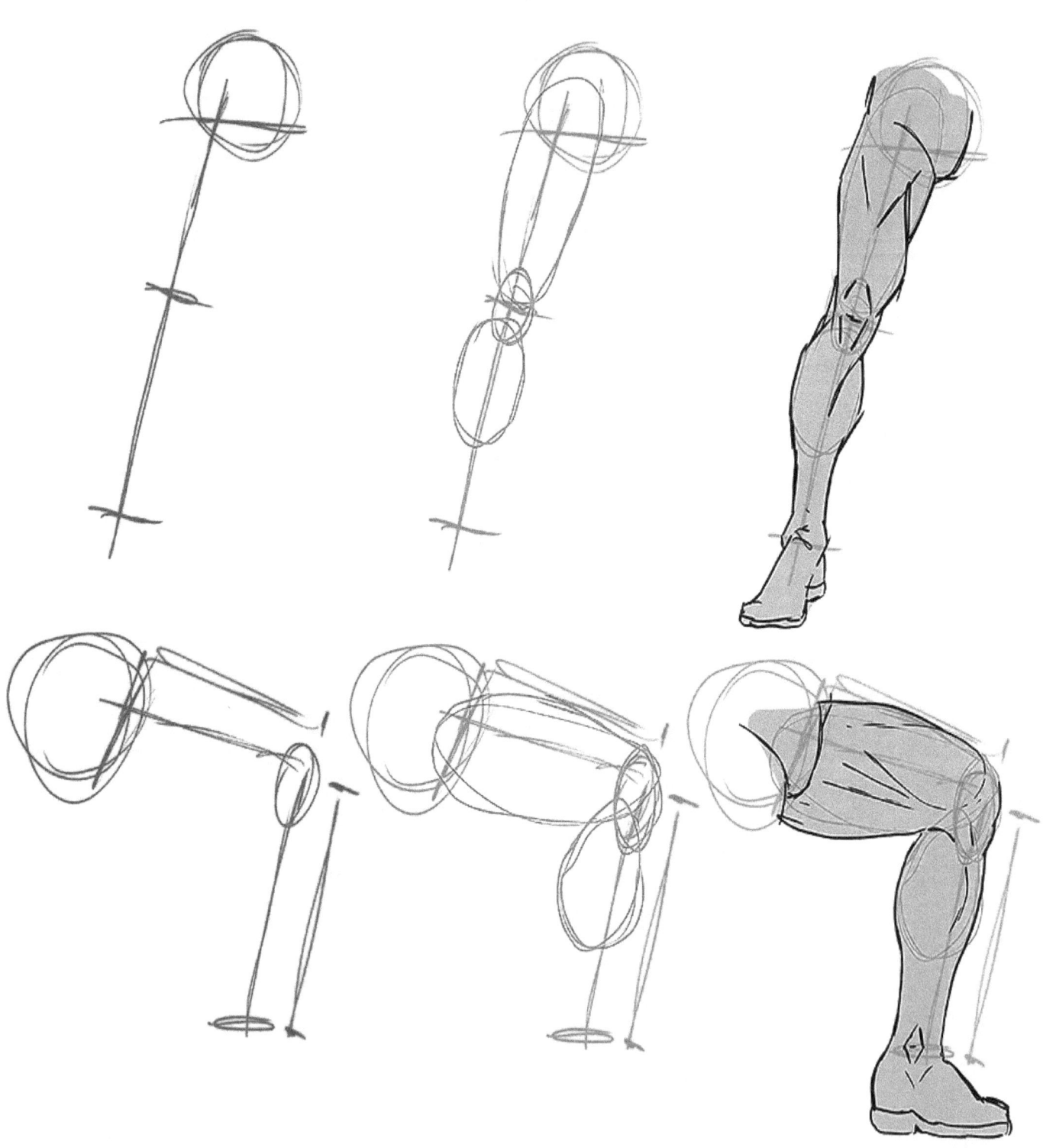

Explain the basic structure

Start with a straight line down the middle to determine the length and movement of the leg.
At the waist, draw two circles or ovals slightly apart at the top. This helps to set the spine.

Split your legs and hips

For each leg, draw a vertical oval or cylinder for the thigh. The waist is large and tapers slightly to the knees.
Draw a small oval or cylinder for the calf under each thigh. The calf muscle extends upward and downward to the ankle.

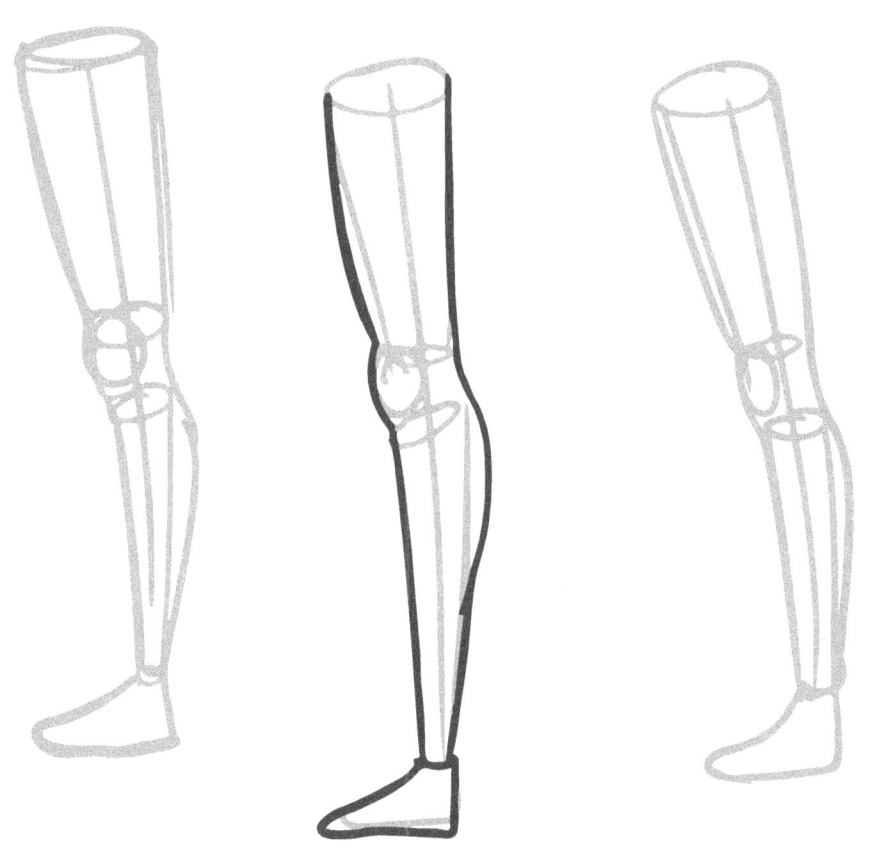

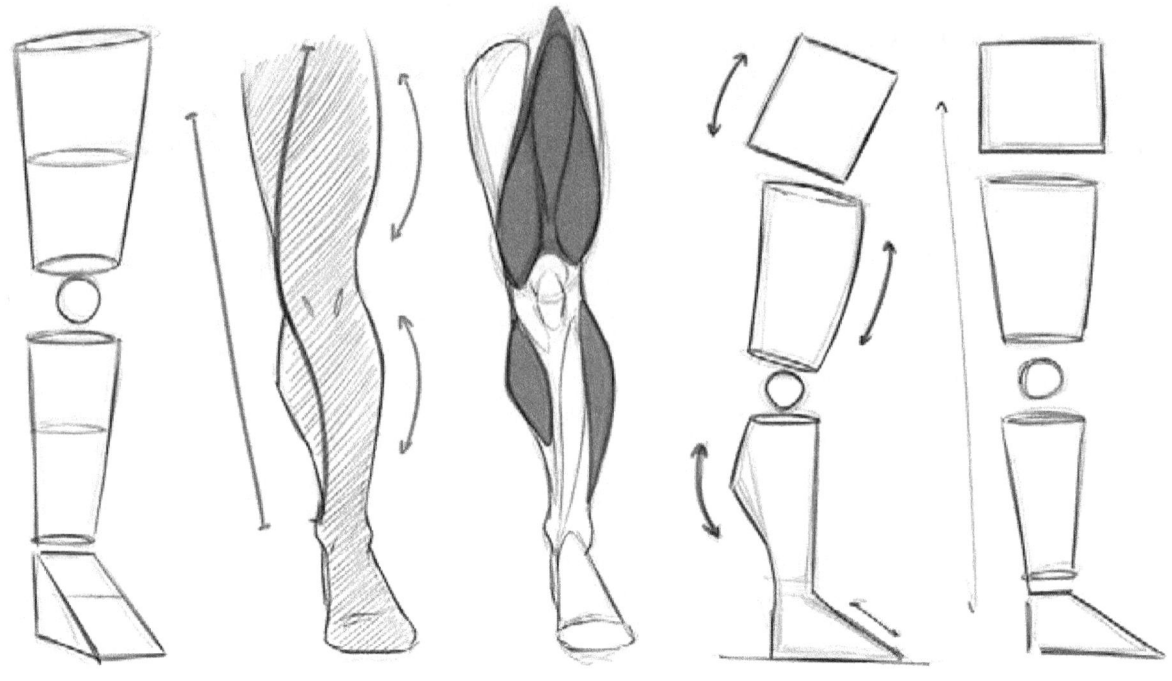

Mark your knees and ankles

At the point where the hip meets the calf, draw a small circle for the knee joint. Draw another small circle for the ankle joint at the base of each calf. This helps with proper positioning and thinking.

Design the legs

Connect the thighs to the calf, keeping them very far apart. The inner side of the calf is usually inward, while the outer side is slightly bent for the calf muscles.
Reduce the size down to the ankle, making sure that the ankle is narrower than the calf.

Add the legs

Pull your feet through the toe grooves. The legs can be drawn in basic shapes (squares or rectangles initially) to guide them.
For more detail, add triangles, hips and ankles.

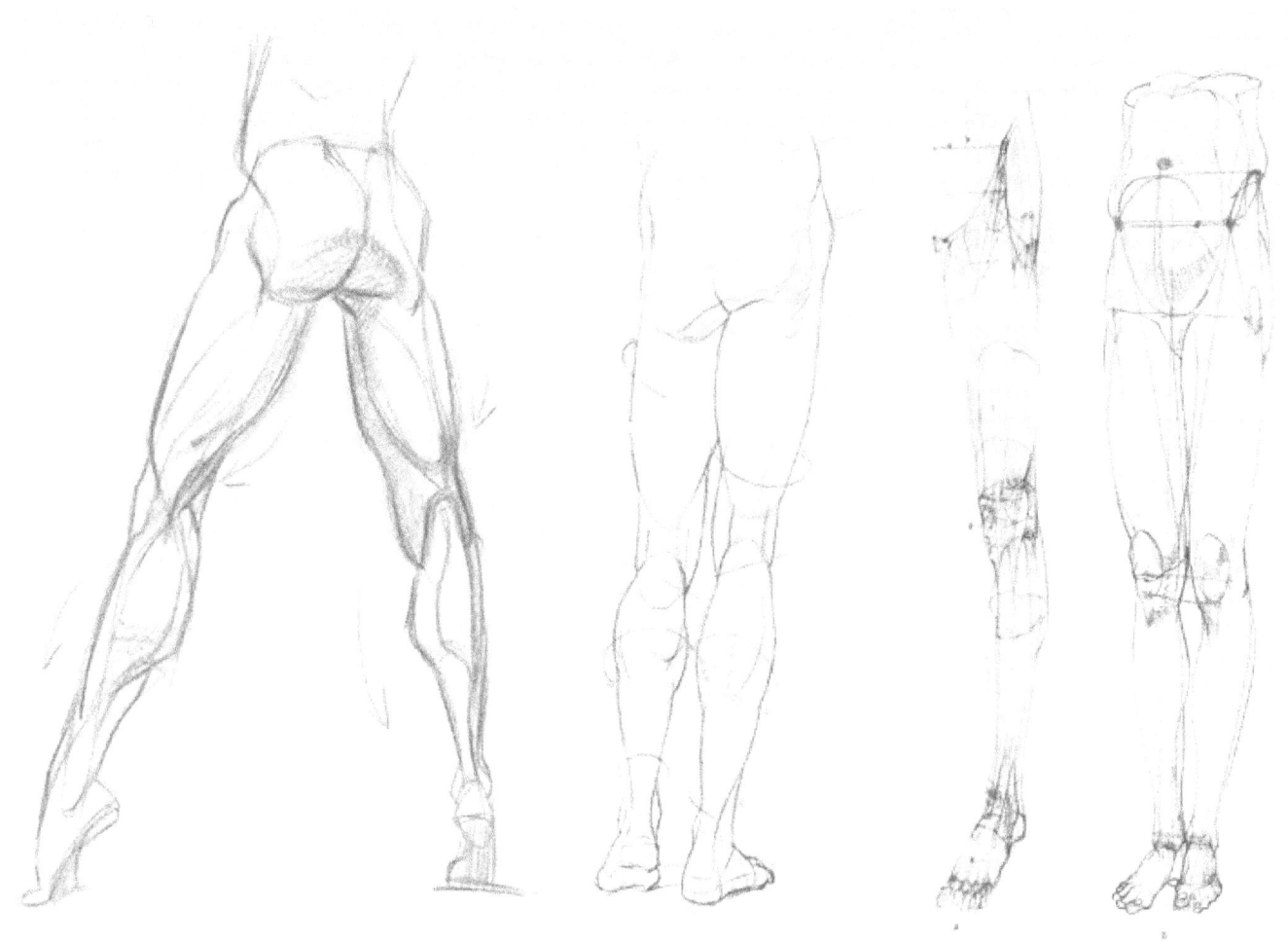

Refine the Outline and Add Muscle Definition

Once the basic shape is complete, refine the outline by adding subtle curves to indicate muscle definition, especially around the thigh and calf.
Emphasize the knee cap and slight indentations around the joints for realism.

Add Details and Shading

Add shading to create depth, focusing on the areas under the knee, around the calf, and where the light source casts shadows.
Draw skin creases at the knee and ankle joints to make the legs look more natural.

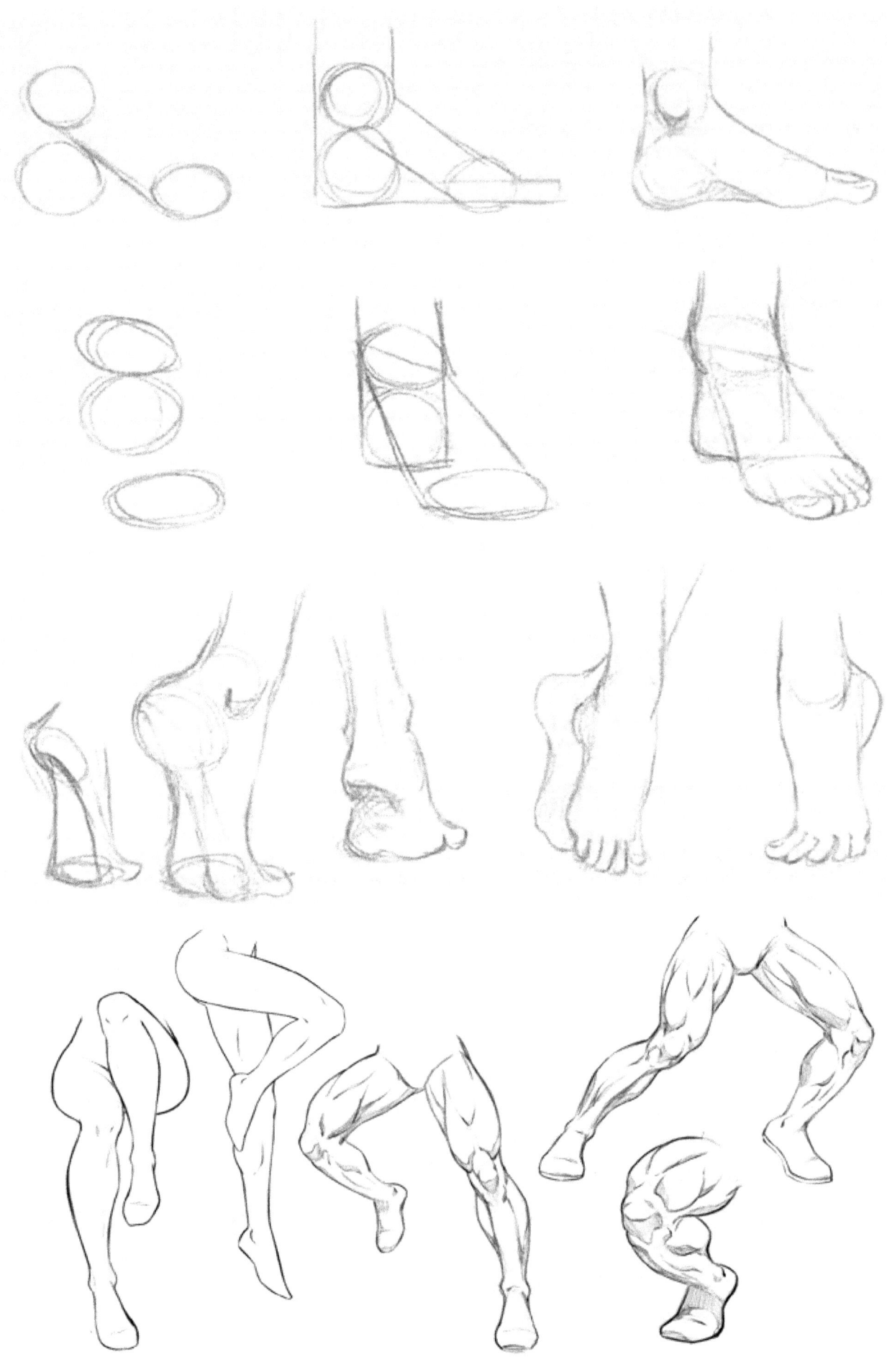

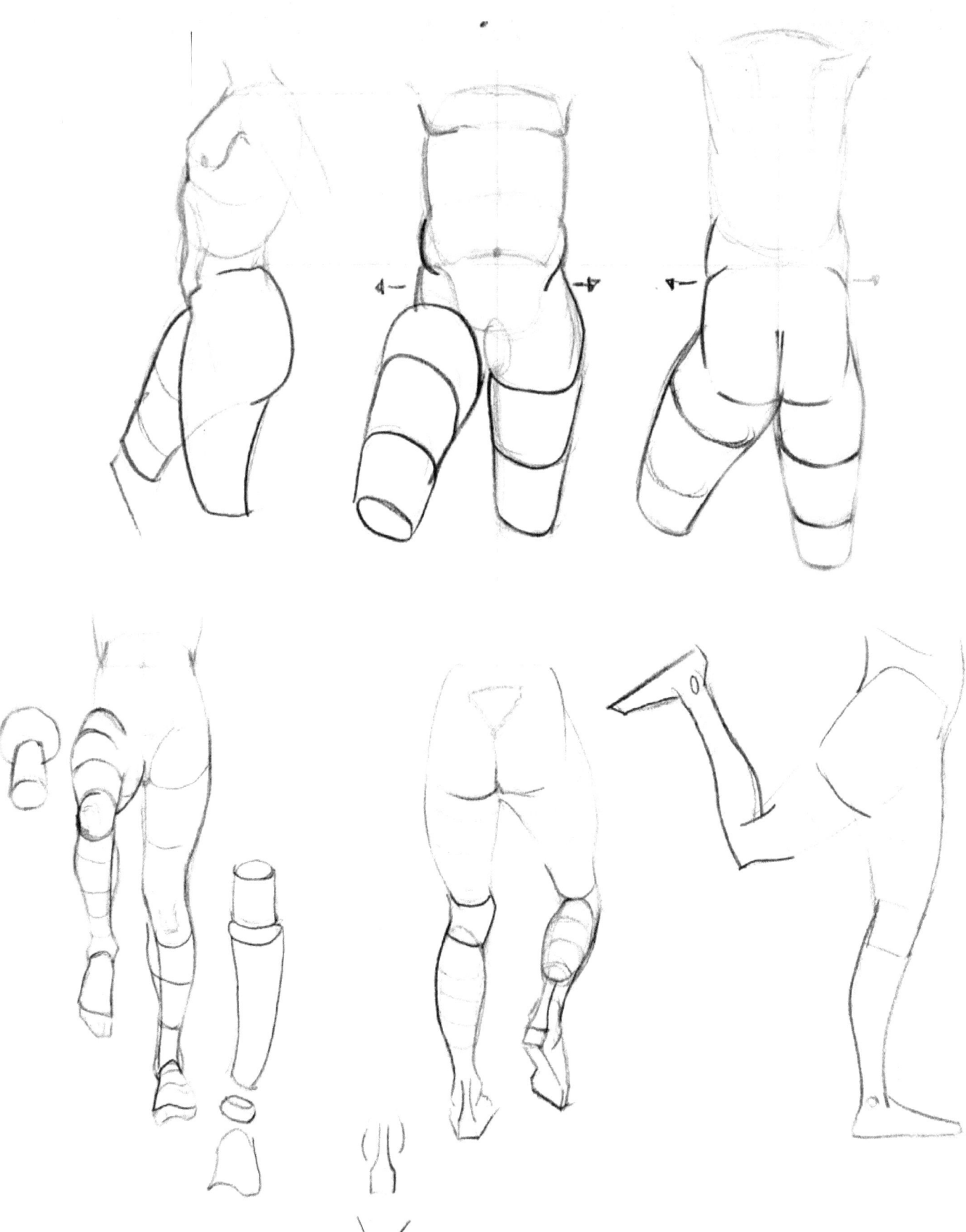

Face painting can be broken down into steps that help in shaping and detailing. Here is a simple guide to get started.

Draw the basic outline of the head

Start with an oval or circle for the head. This will be the top of the chapter.
Add a horizontal guideline in the middle to help create evenness, and a horizontal line in the middle to mark the eyes.

Split the face to fit

From the eye, divide the face into three equal parts.
Upper part: from the top of the head to the brow line.
Middle section: from brow line to base of nose.
Lower part: from the nose to the bottom of the thigh

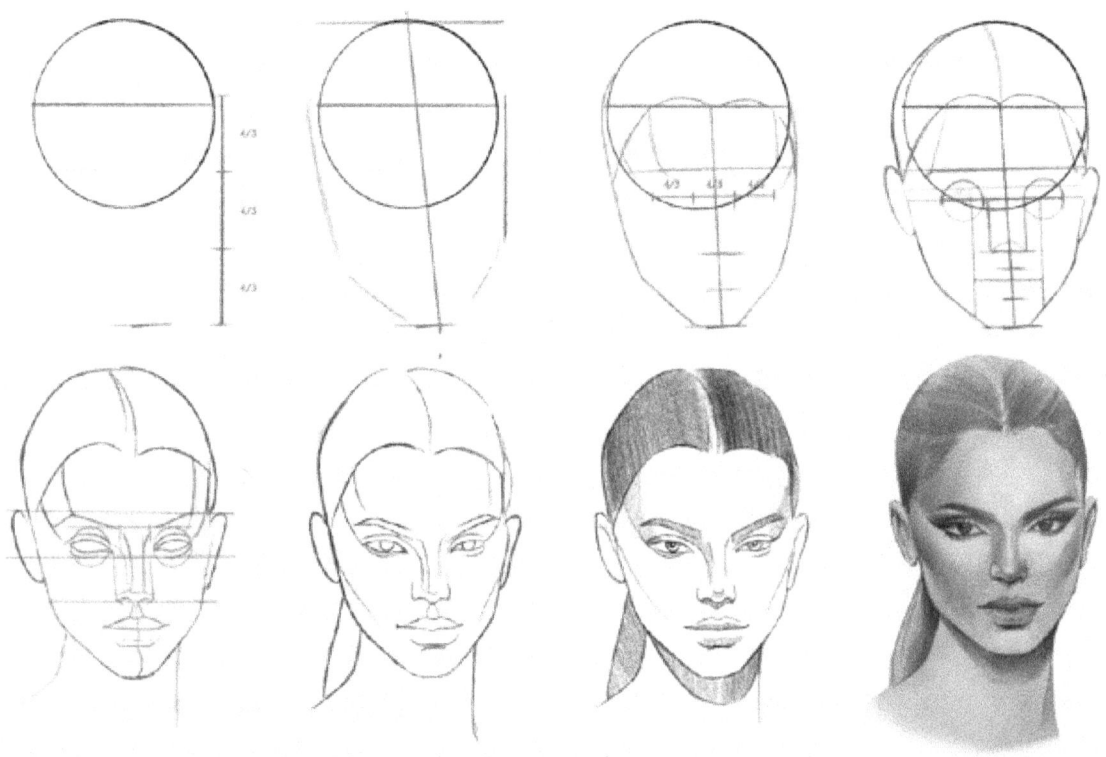

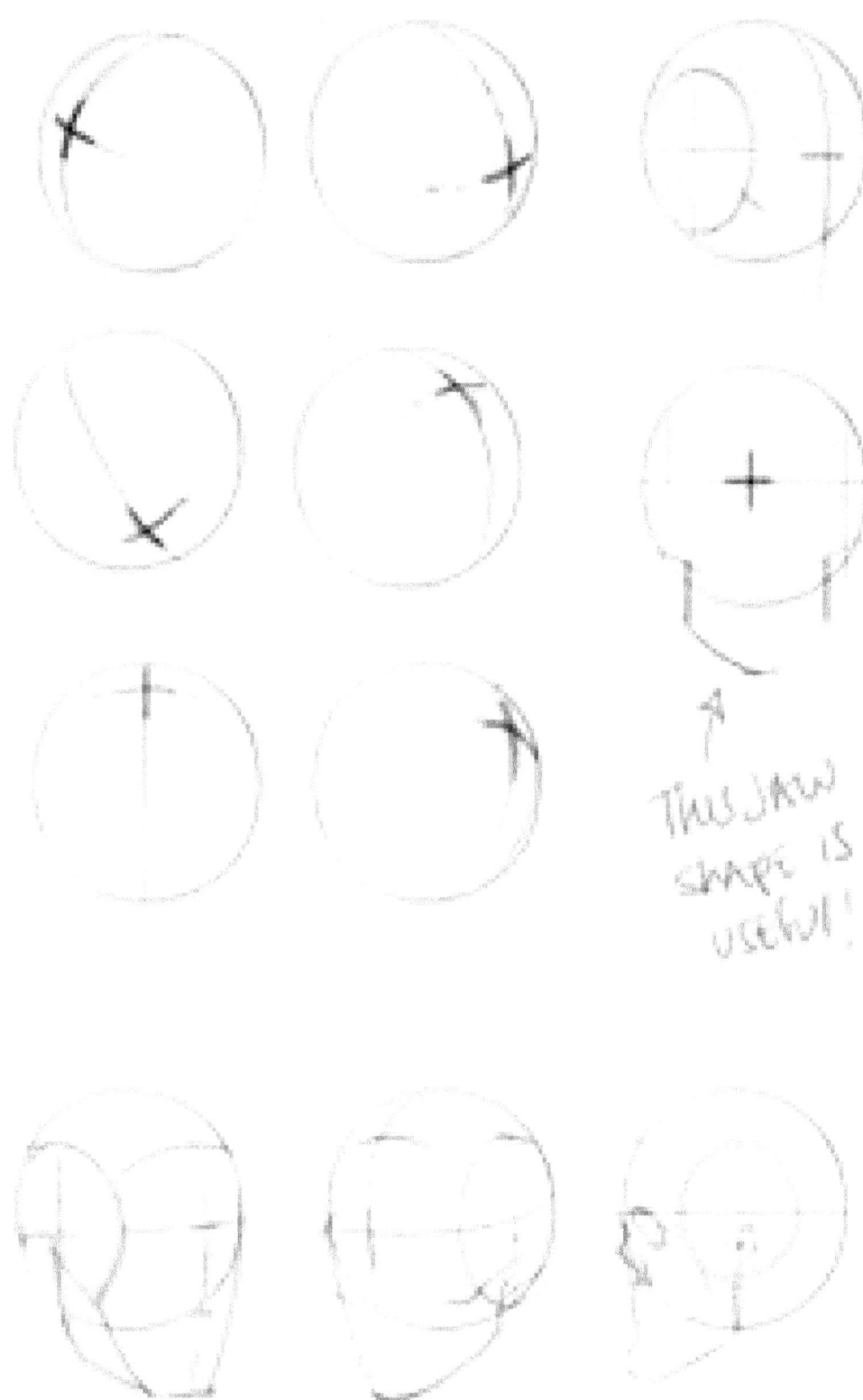

↑
THIS JAW
shape is
useful!

Place the Eyes

On the eye line, draw two almond shapes for the eyes, spaced about an eye's width apart.
Add eyelids and sketch in the iris and pupil. Remember that the eyes are not full circles; they're partially covered by the eyelids.

Draw the Nose

On the nose line, draw the nose shape. Start with a small circle at the tip of the nose, then add two smaller circles on either side for the nostrils. Shape the bridge of the nose up to the brow line, adjusting for different nose shapes if desired.

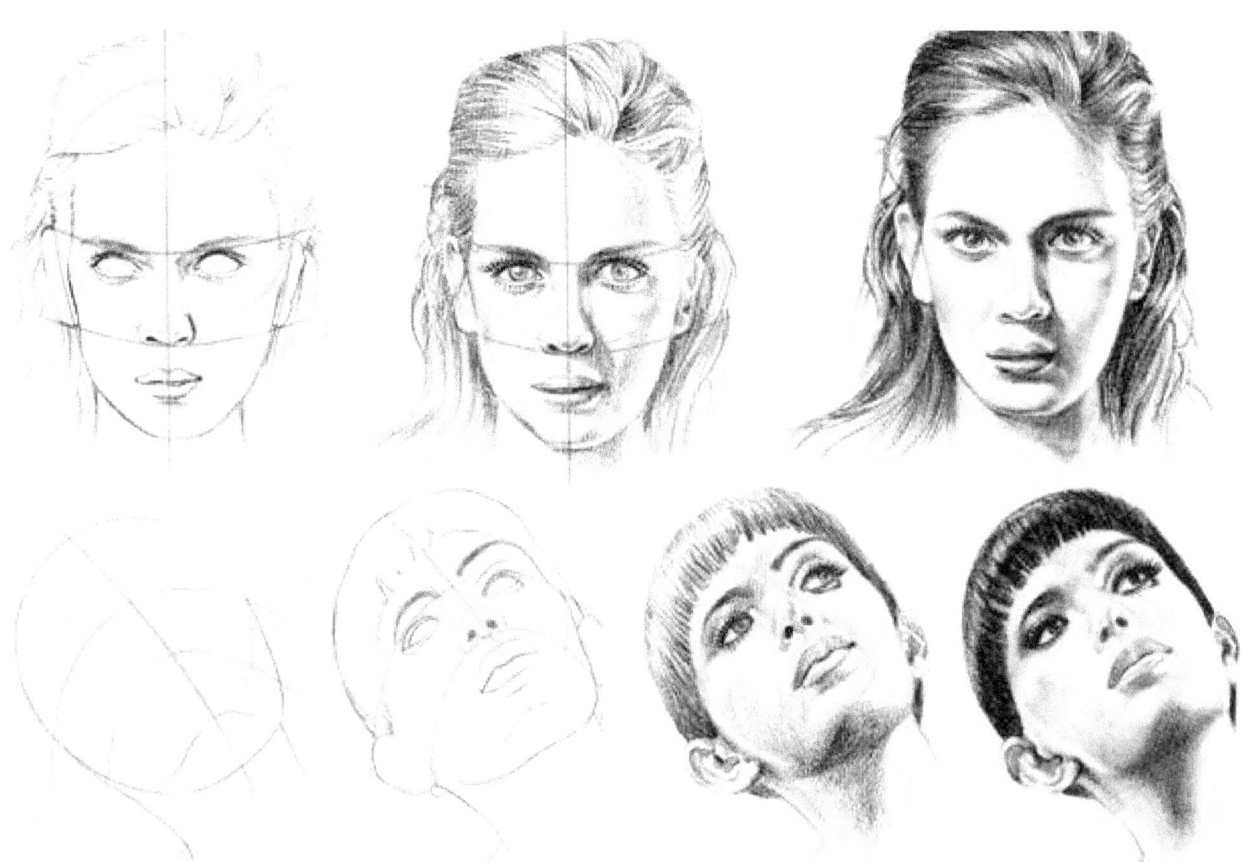

Pull your face together

Draw a line for the mouth area between nose and chin.
Start with circular lines for your upper lip and slightly fuller lines for your lower lip.
Remember to generally keep the brow width in line with the center of the eye.

Keep your ears open

The top of the ear meets the eye and the bottom of the ear meets the nose.
Draw any curves in the ears, and add details, such as veins.

Add eye and hair lines

Draw an eyebrow on your eyes. Depending on the expression, they can be thin, thick, square or straight.
For the hairline, draw a horizontal line just above the eye line. Next, add the hair considering how it falls naturally across the face.

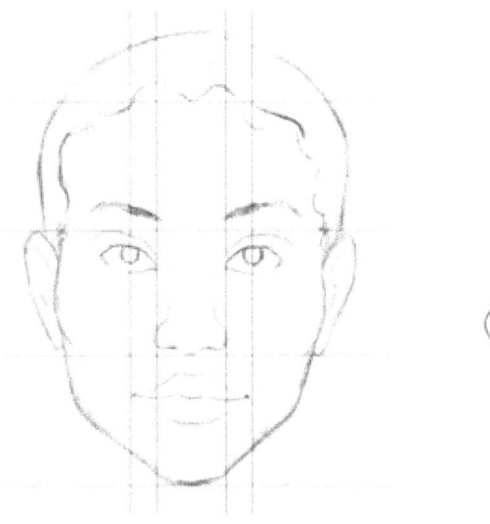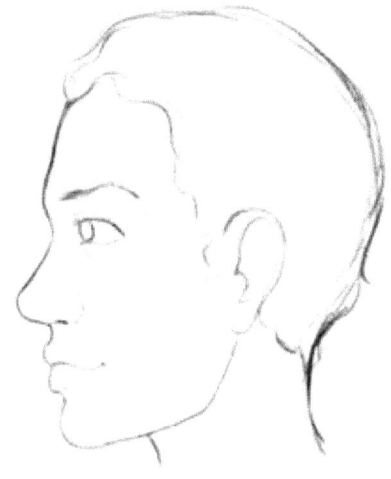

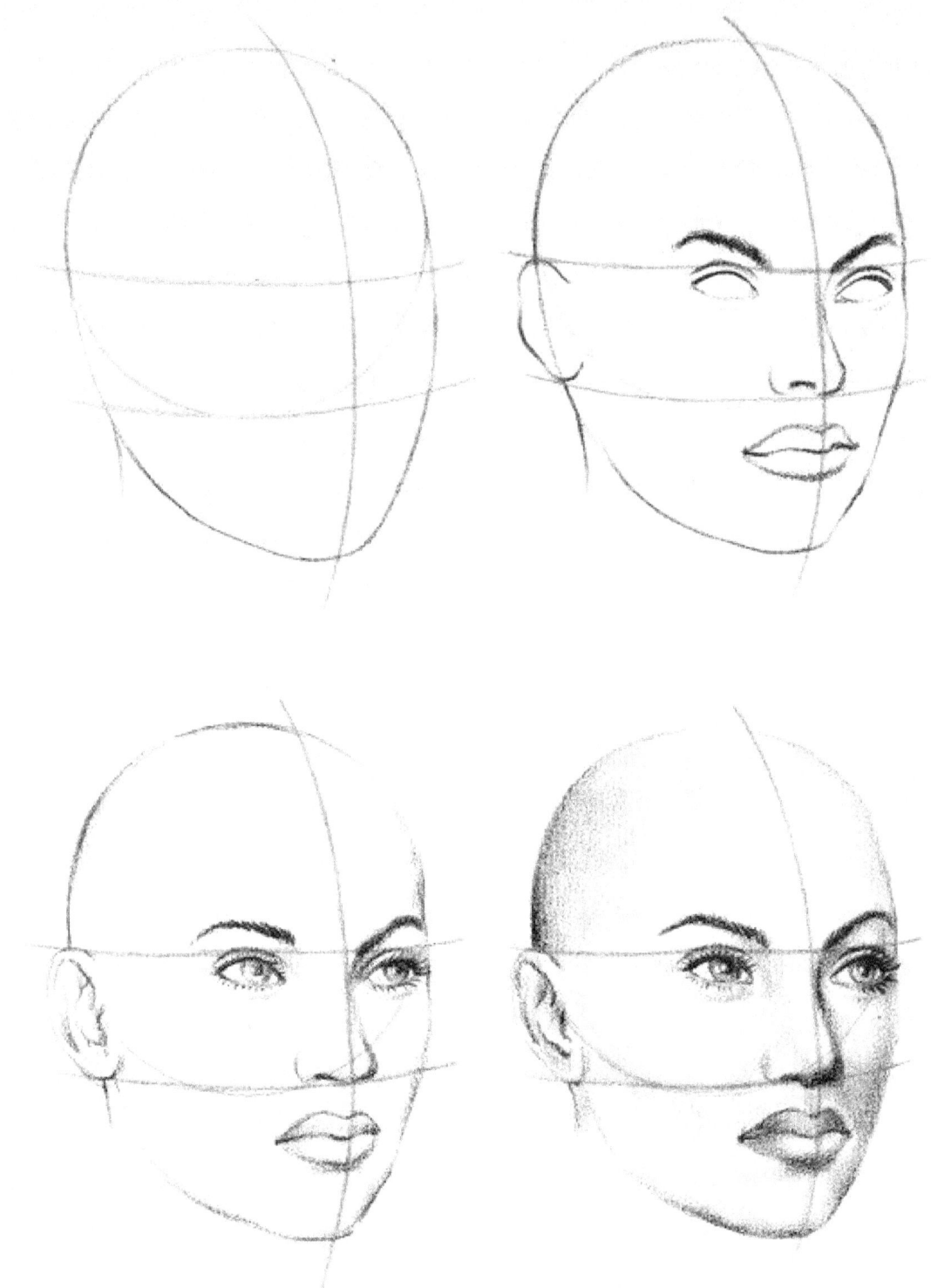

Clean it up and add details

Add details like wrinkles, creases under the eyes, and fine lines around the mouth and nose for authenticity.
Carefully define the contours of your face, smooth out any rough lines and define your chin.

Shadow for depth

Create depth by adding shadow to the eye, nose, and mouth areas. For example, shadows under the nose, under the lower lip, and around the edges of the mouth.
Focus on the shadows around the cheekbones and forehead and use lighter dark tones to define the contours of the face.

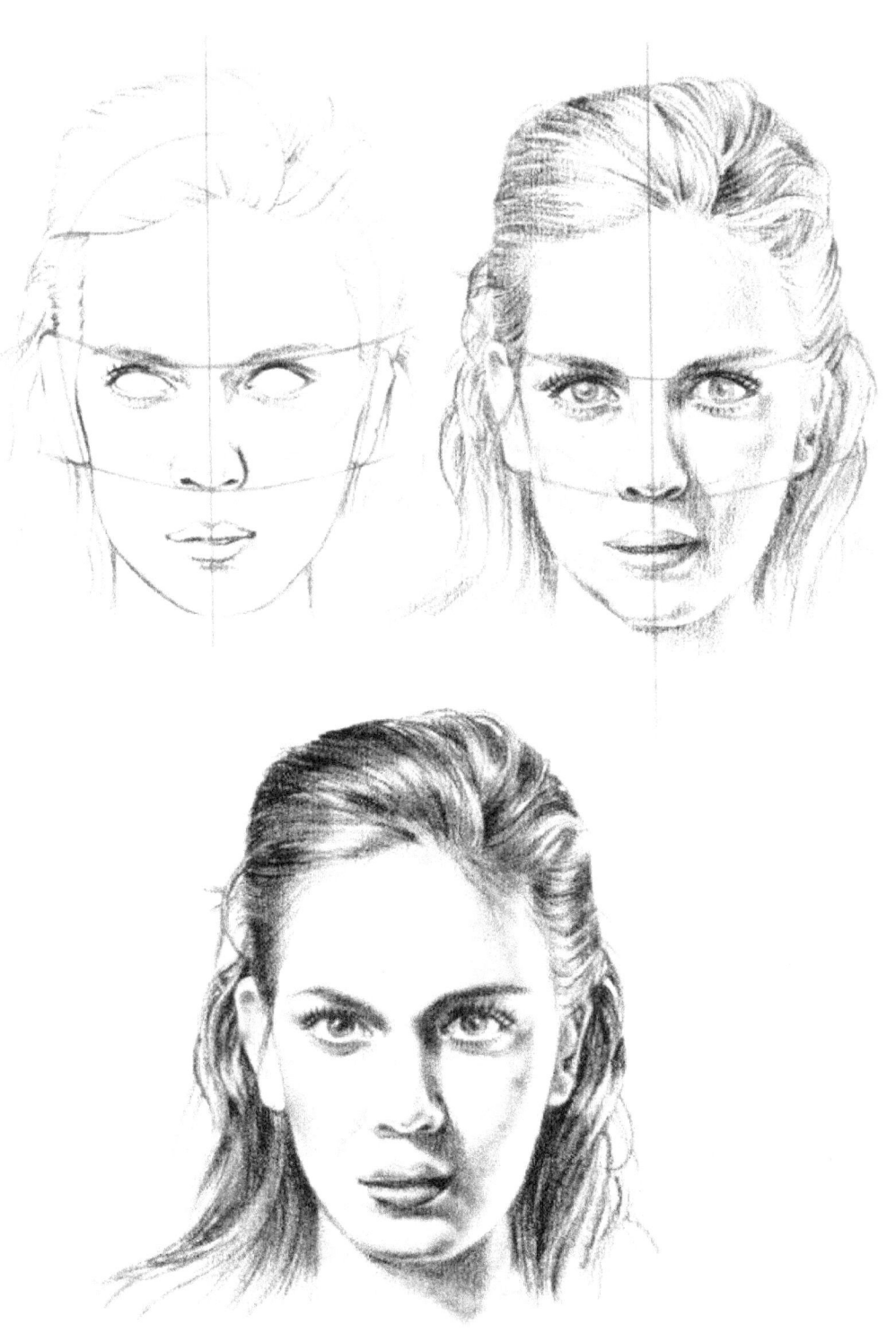

Practice Different Angles and Expressions

Once you're comfortable with the basics, try drawing faces at different angles and with various expressions. This will help you understand facial proportions and improve your overall skills

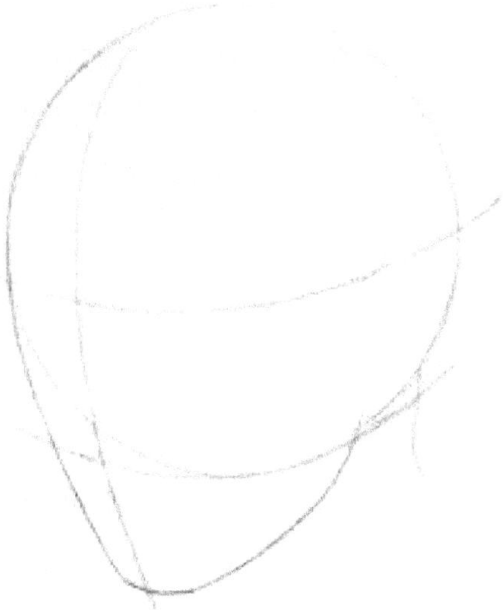

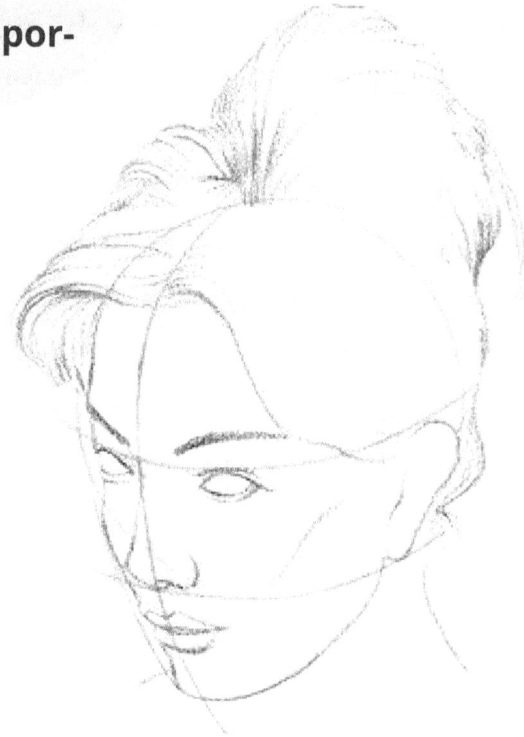

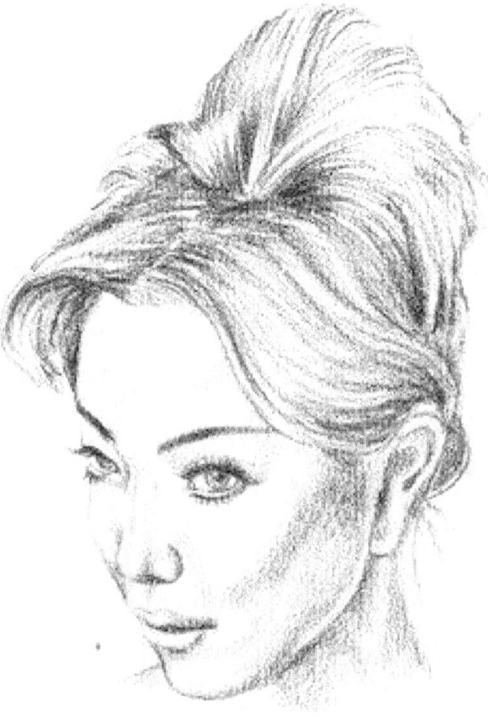

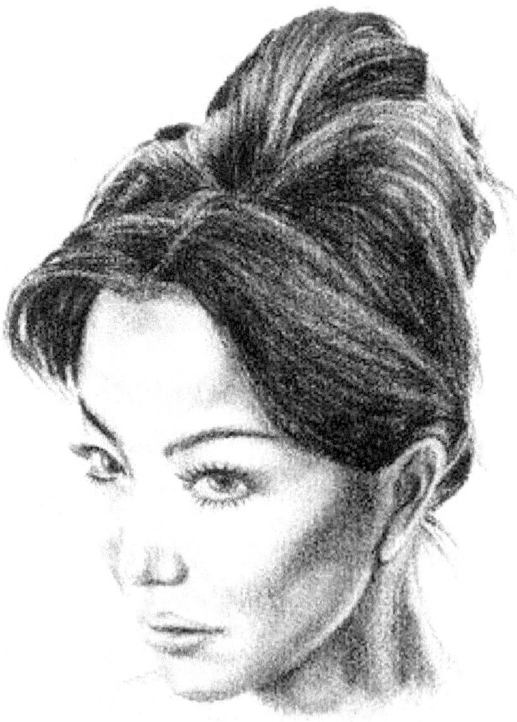

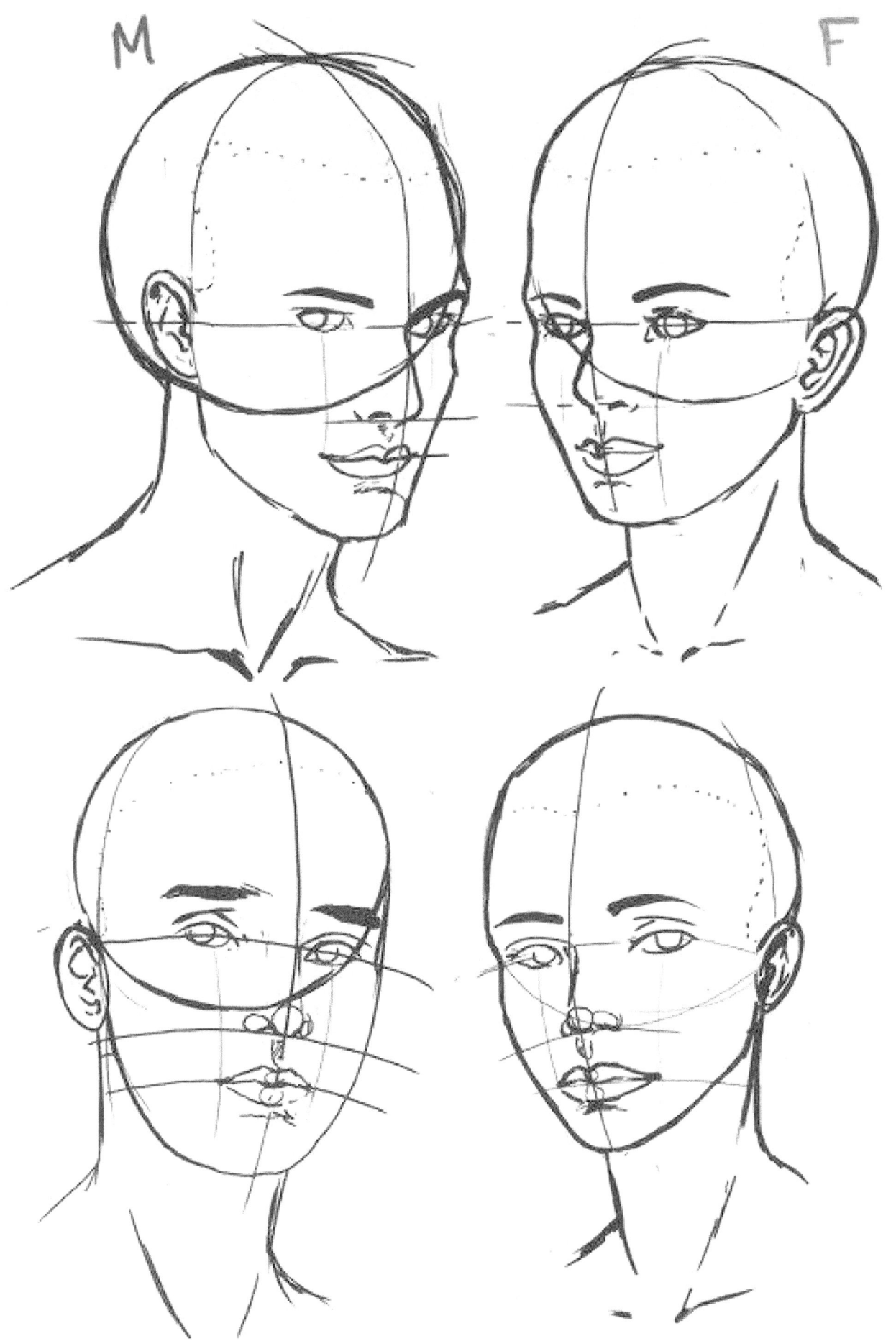
M

F

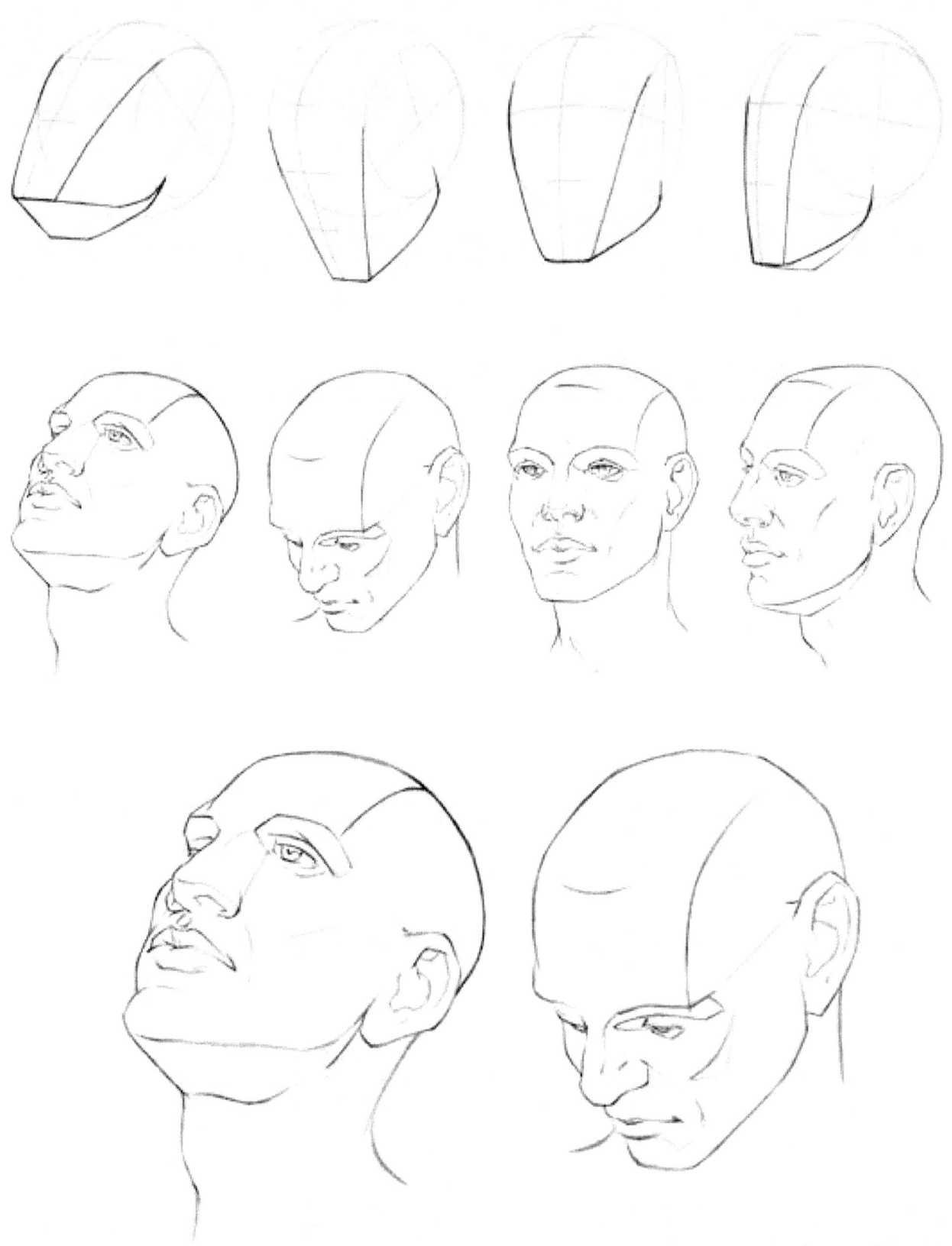

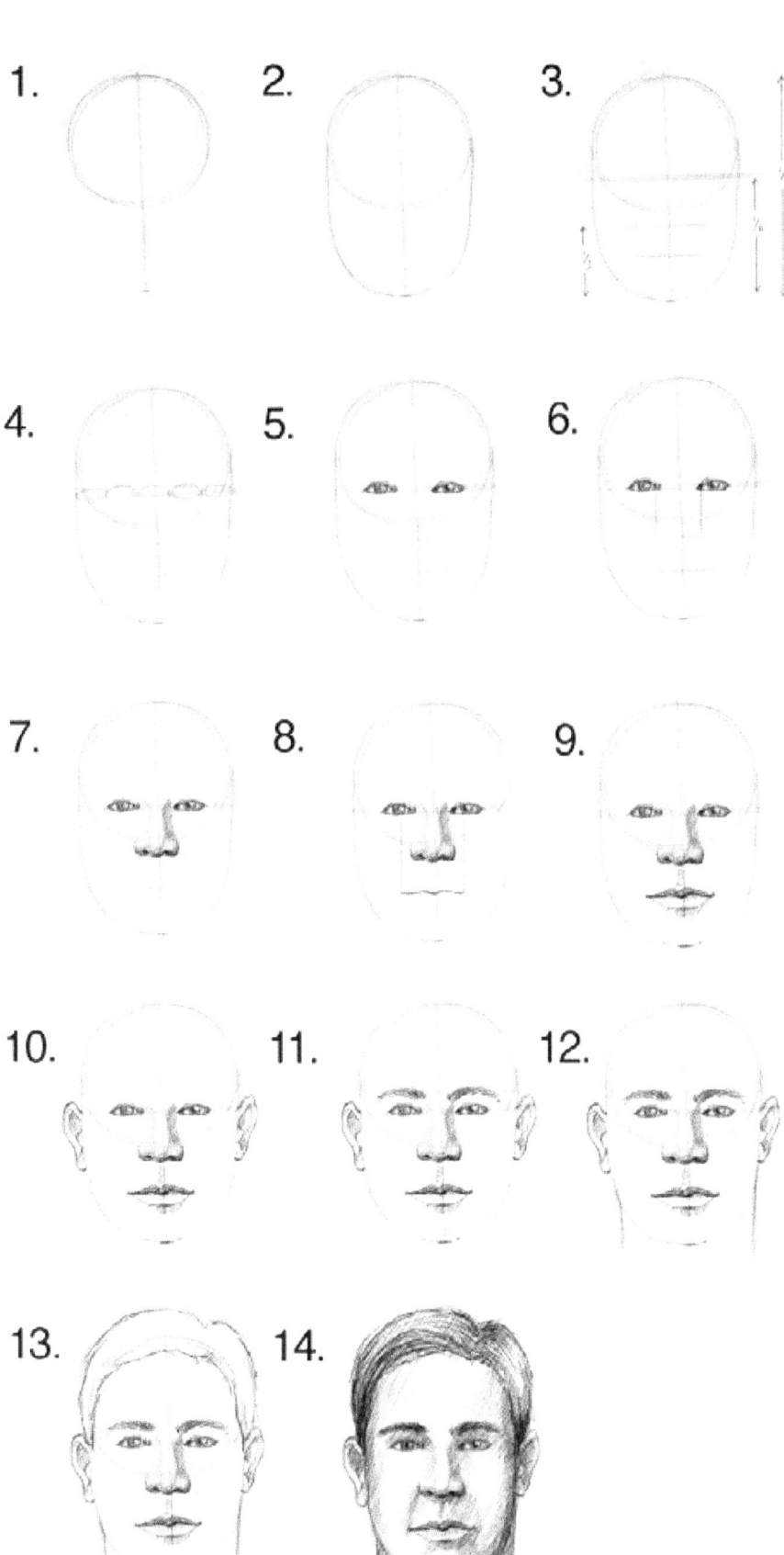

1.

2.

3.

4.

5.

6.

7.

8.

9.

10.

11.

12.

13.

14.

YOUR TURN NOW

Drawing a nose can be challenging, but by breaking it into simple shapes and focusing on the structure, you can capture it accurately. Here's a step-by-step guide:

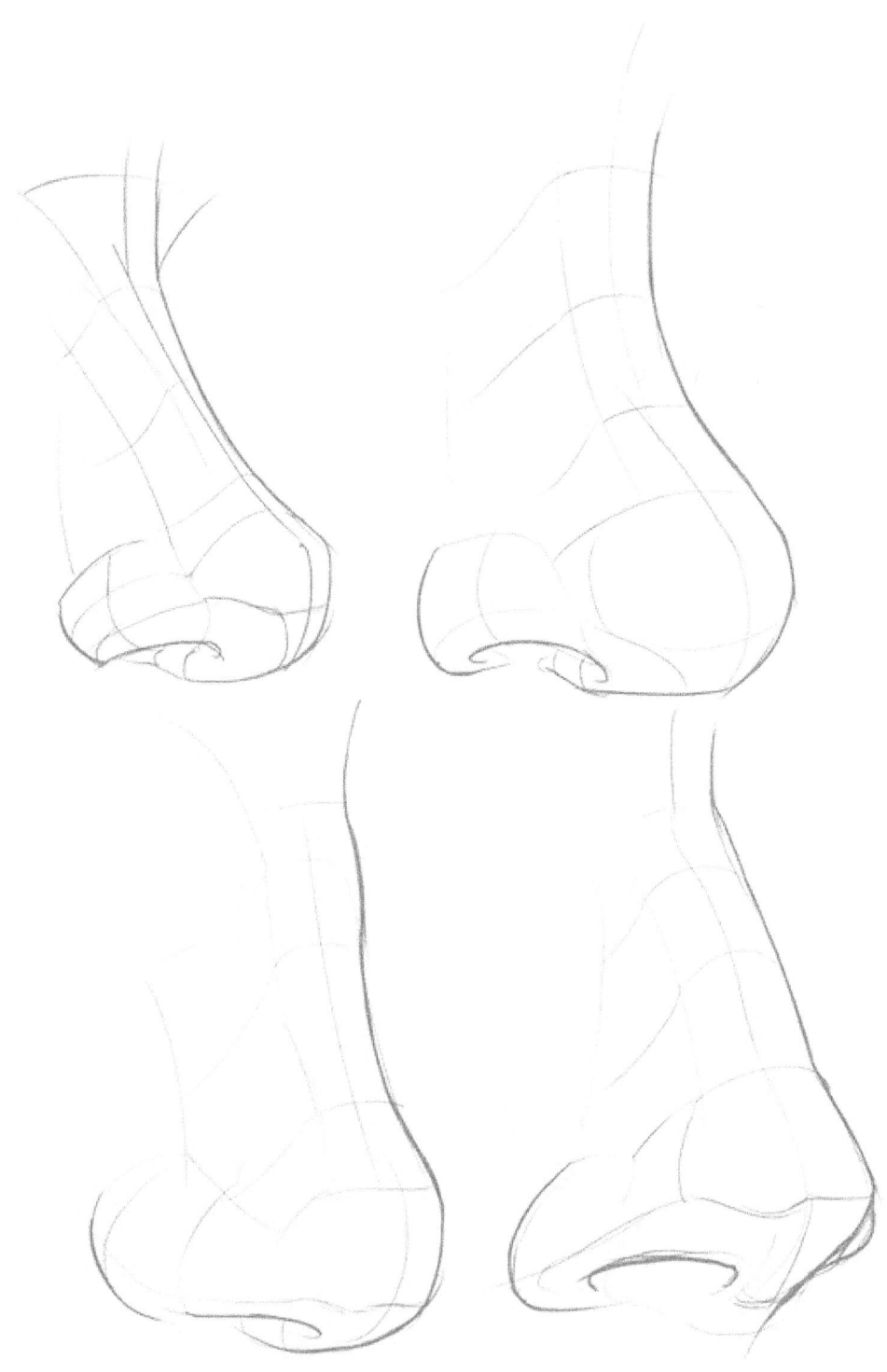

Start with Basic Design

Draw a circle for the tip of the nose. This circle helps you determine its size and placement.

Draw two smaller circles for the noses on either side of the circle. These curves will help with placement and give the nose a perfect base.

Gently connect the circles with circular braids to get the base of your nose.

Add the nasal bridge

Starting from the large circle on the forearm, draw two lines up to where your eyes are. These lines can be straight or slightly curved depending on the nose shape you are drawing.

The bridge generally gets narrower as you climb, so the lines should be tapered to the eye.

Define the nasal muscles

Draw two "heart" or "C" shaped lines to create a nostril around the smaller sections. Make sure the nose is parallel to the mouth and evenly spaced.

Use small stitches to connect your nose to the tip of your nose, defining the sides of your nose.

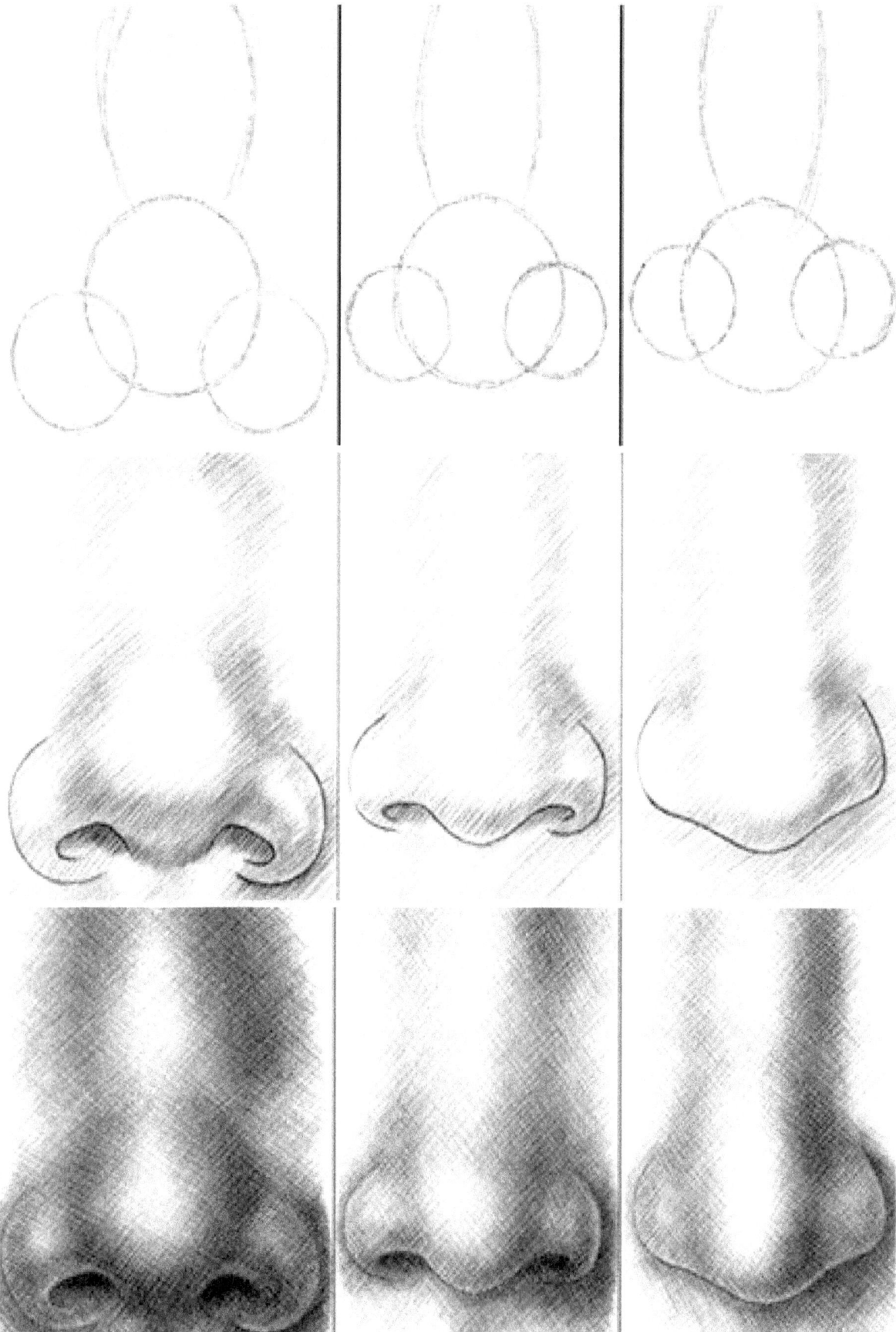

Shape of the oral wing (Alae) .

Extend slightly round from each nostril to form a "wing" on the nose (outer edge).
These should blend well into the mouth and are usually more pronounced on the floor near the nose.

Add Shading to create Depth

Create depth by shading the sides of the bridge. The bridge of the nose usually has shaded edges that give it a three-dimensional appearance. Shading around the tip of the nose and under the tip of the nose to make it look more realistic.

Adding a soft shadow to the "wings" of the nose adds to it.

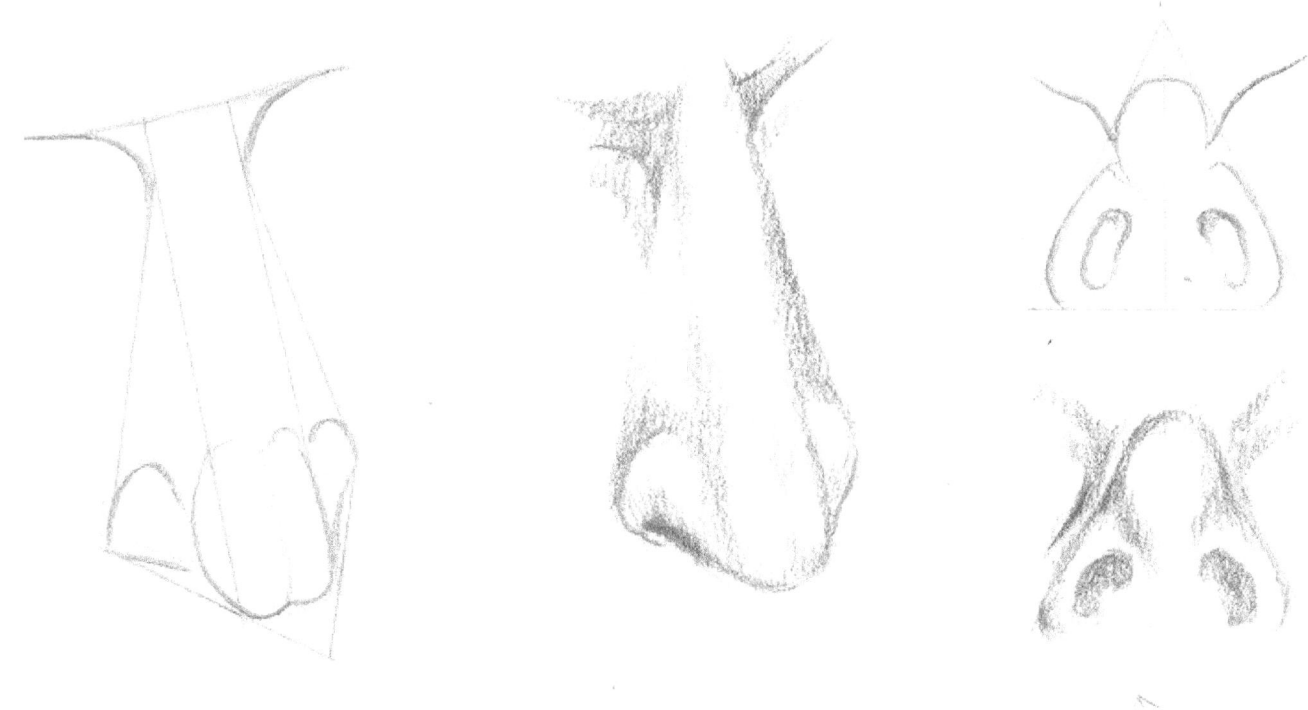

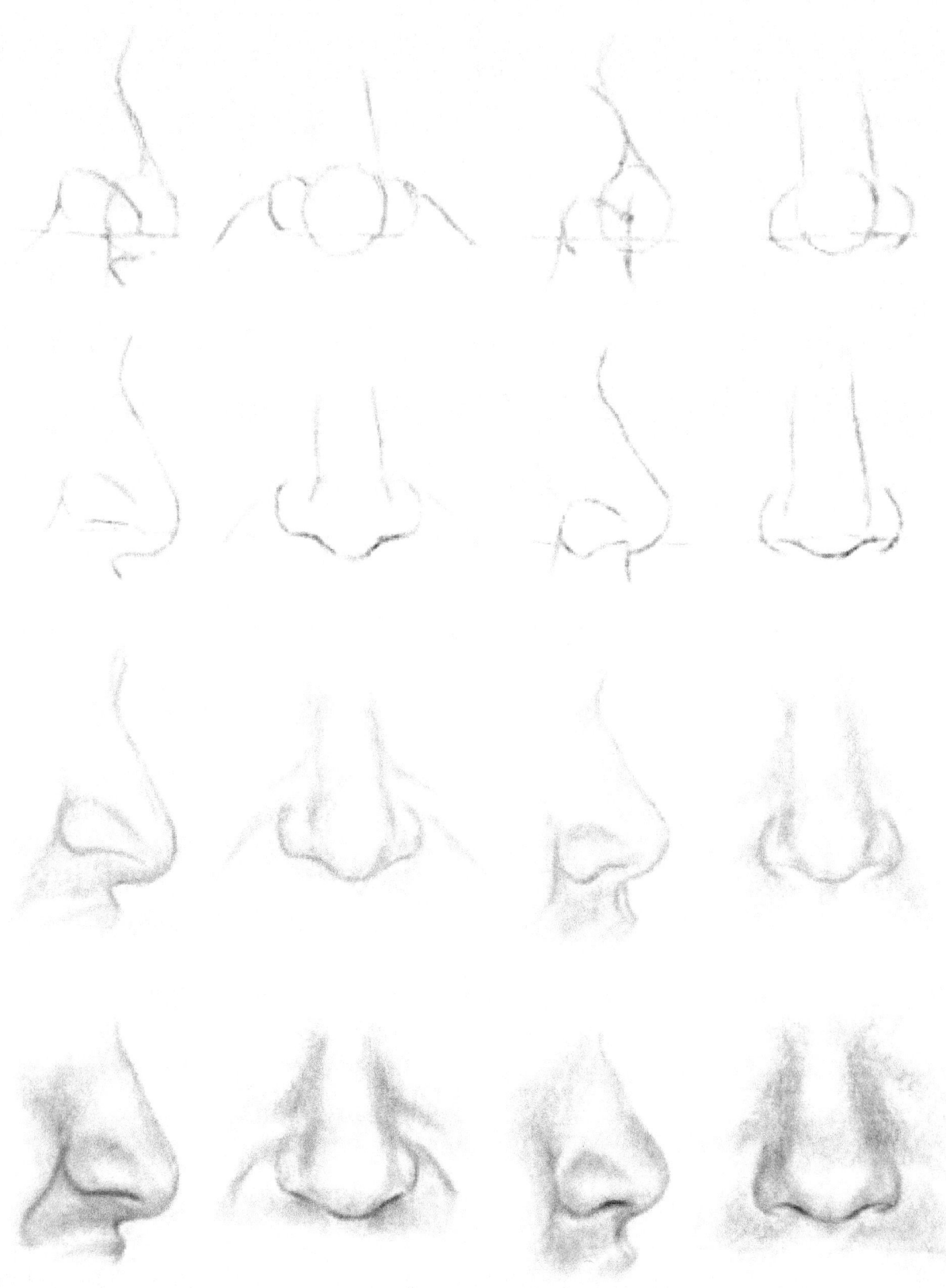

Different Angles

When drawing the nose from different angles, focus on how the shapes change:

Profile View: The nose bridge becomes more prominent, and the tip and nostrils are more curved.

3/4 View: One nostril will be more visible, and the bridge line will curve toward the visible nostril.

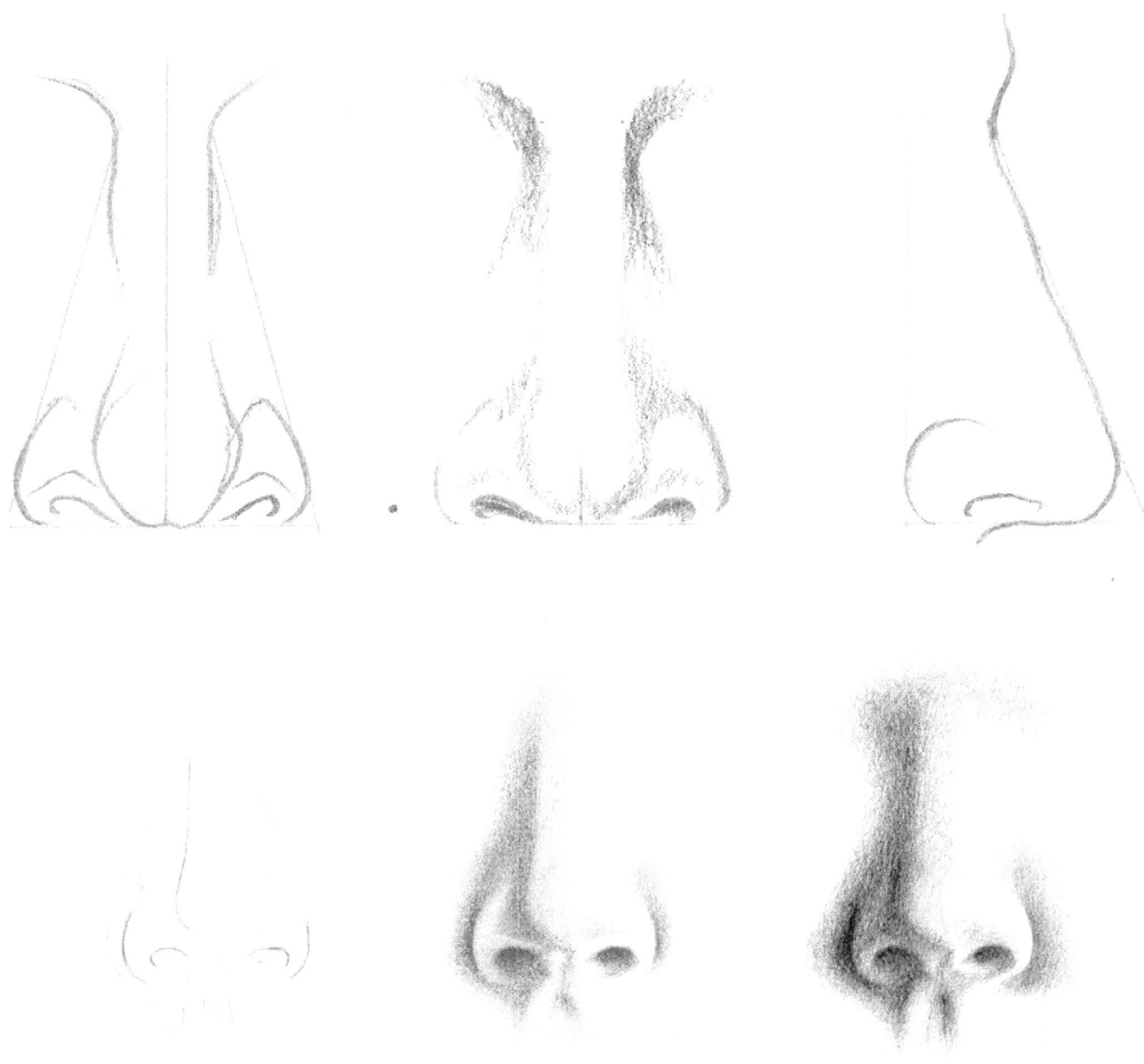

YOUR TURN NOW

YOUR TURN NOW

If you want to create a smaller face, you can make some simple changes to look great. Here's how to draw a simple little face.

Drag the center line

Draw a short horizontal line for the line where the lip meets. This determines the overall width, making the face appear smaller. Keep your nose down and narrower than your eyes.

Thin your lips

Draw a gentle "M" shape for the upper lip, but keep it subtle and understated for the look.
Create a light curl on the lower lip, keeping it narrow and curved without being too tight.

Soften the shadows and details

Slight shadows and avoid harsh contrasts. This makes the face softer and more subtle.
Reduce the number of dots that are open to shape the lips, as too many dots will make the lips look fuller.

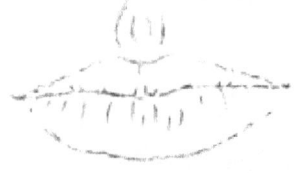 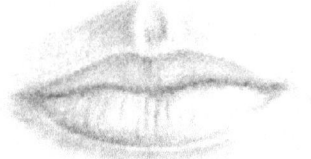 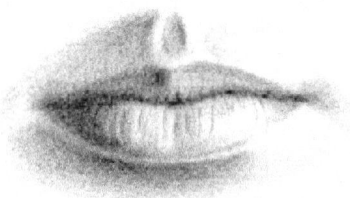

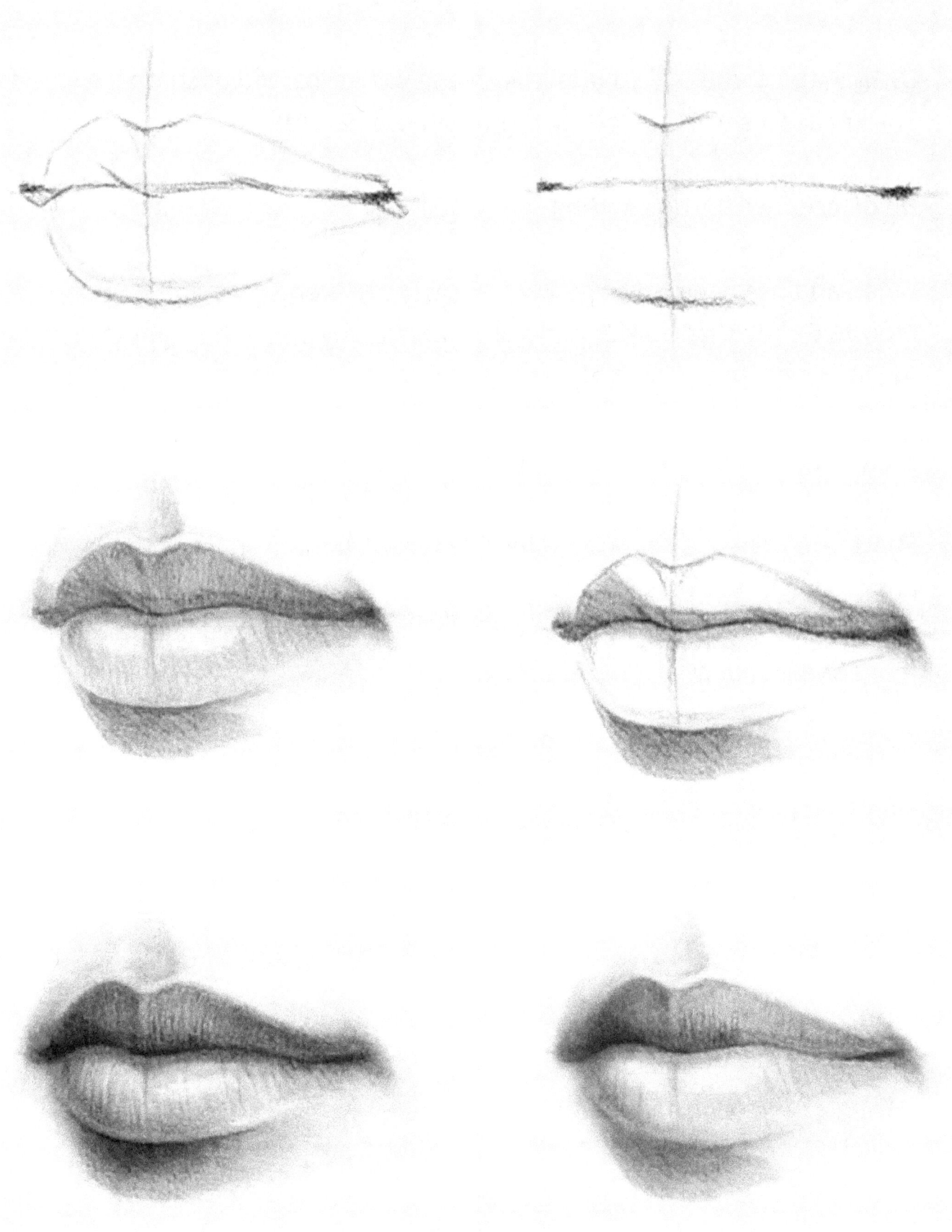

Round the corners

Draw in the corners of your face with a few lines instead of sharp lines. This makes a small face look softer and more natural.

Be discreet with the shading

When adding shading, use gentle transitions to blend your lips in your mouth. Gently shade around the brow and subtly apply the highlights on the lower lips to add a bit of volume.

Make Adjustments in the Proportions

Short faces generally support a flexible face structure, so adjust the width and thickness to fit the face naturally.
These adjustments should give you a smaller, more refined facial profile that appears softer and more balanced.

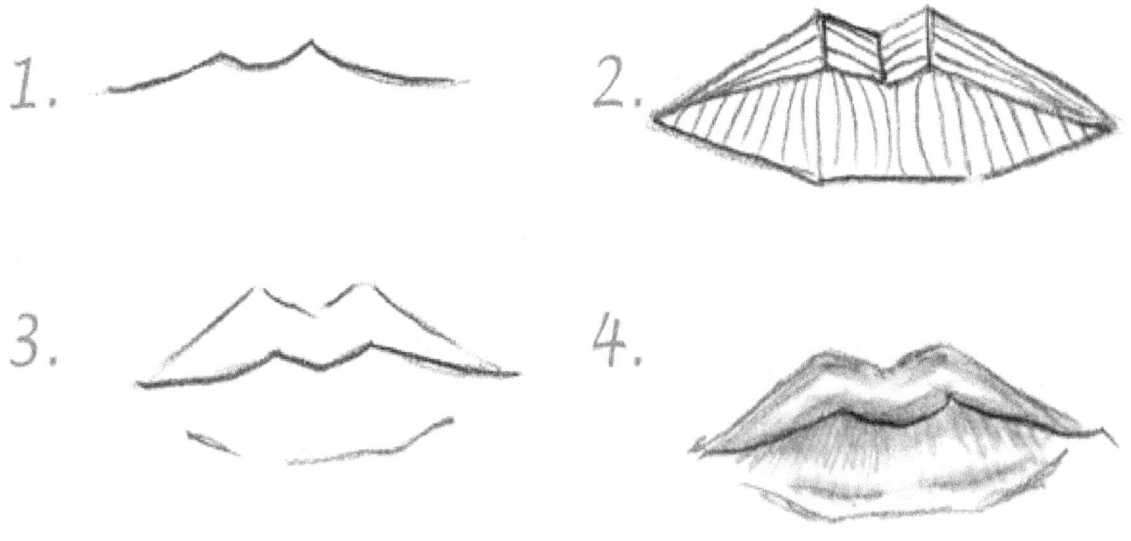

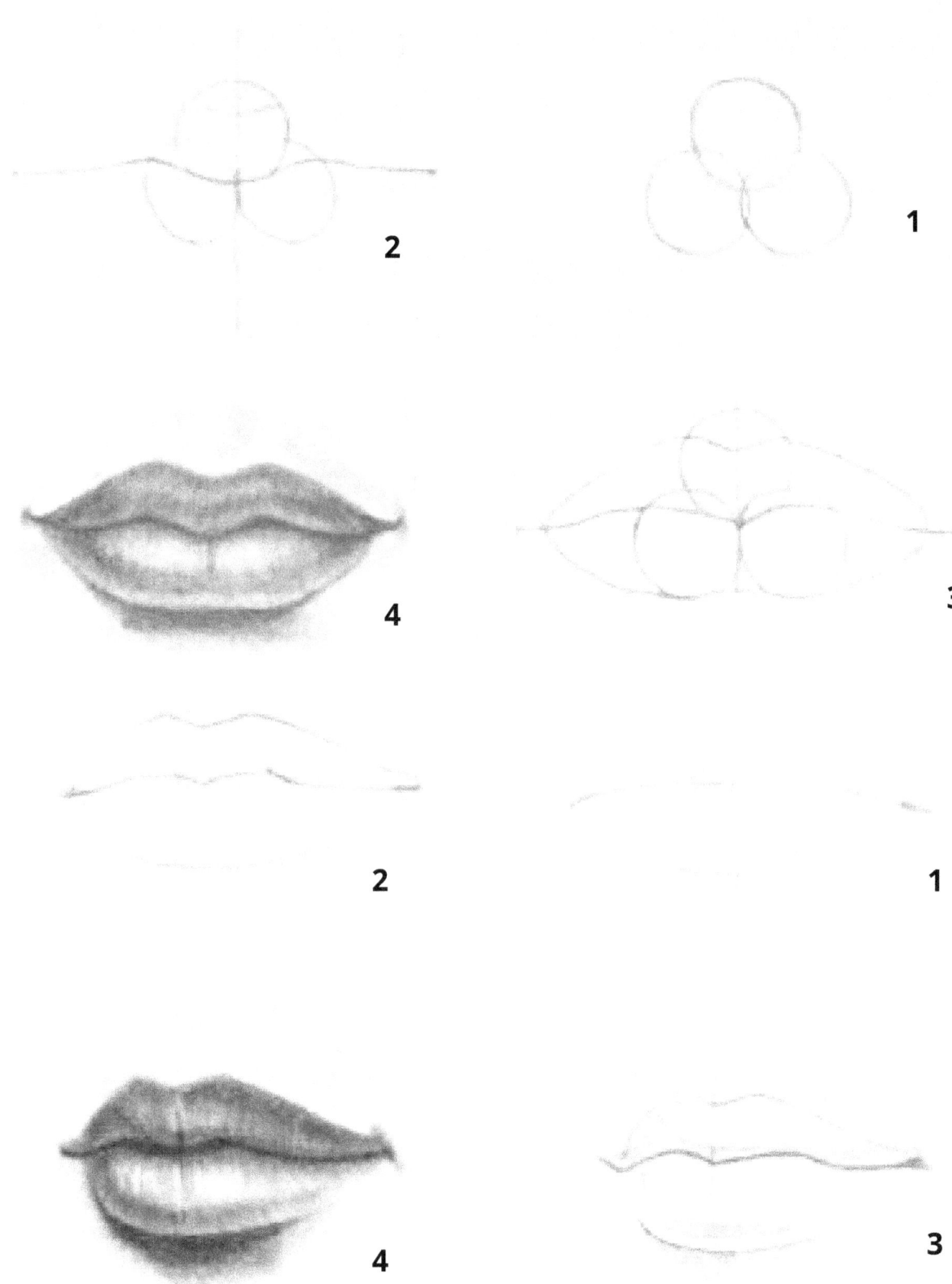

2

1

4

3

2

1

4

3

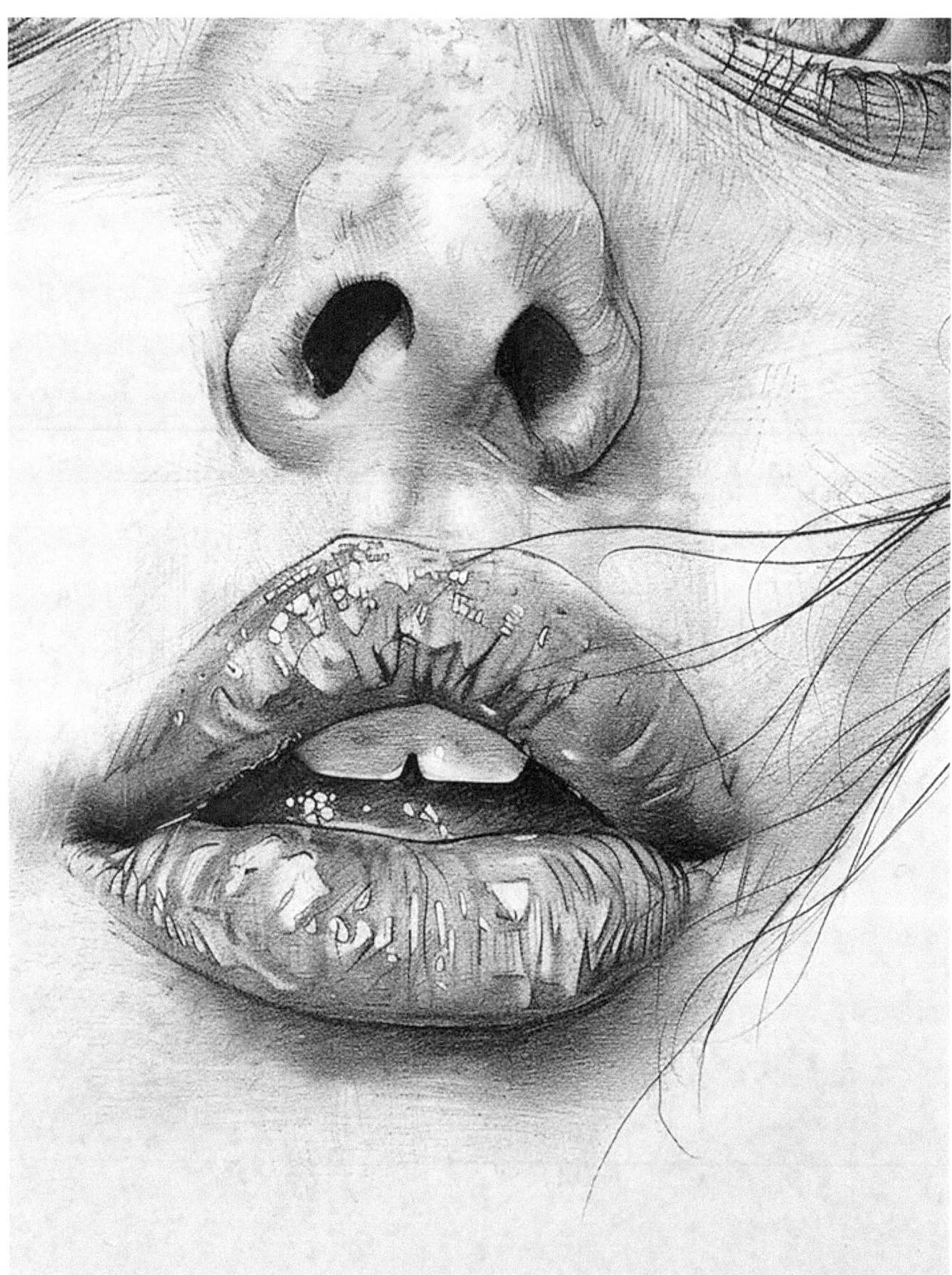

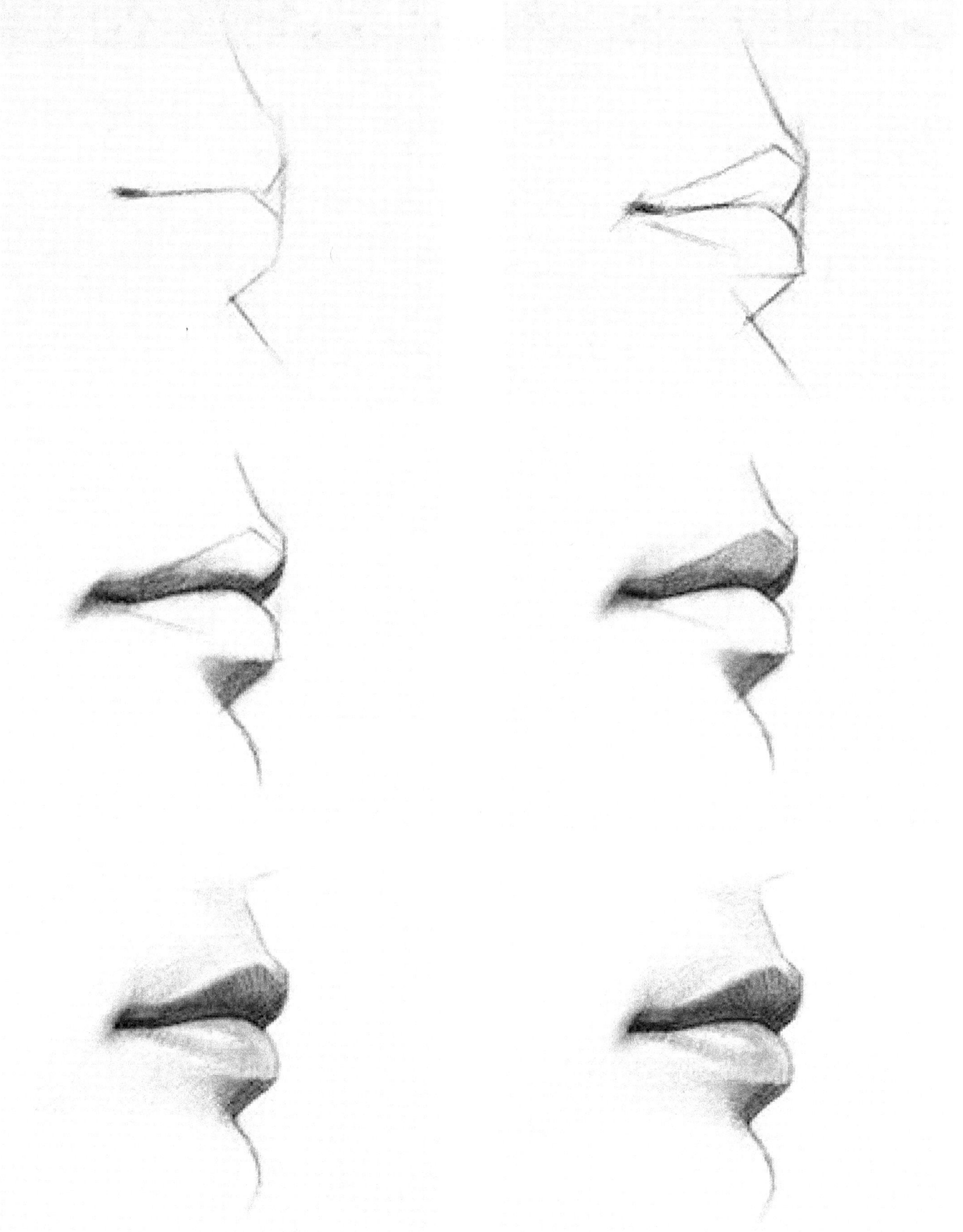

This image provides a helpful step-by-step guide to piercing the ears with precise dimensions and real detail. Here is a breakdown of the process based on what is shown.

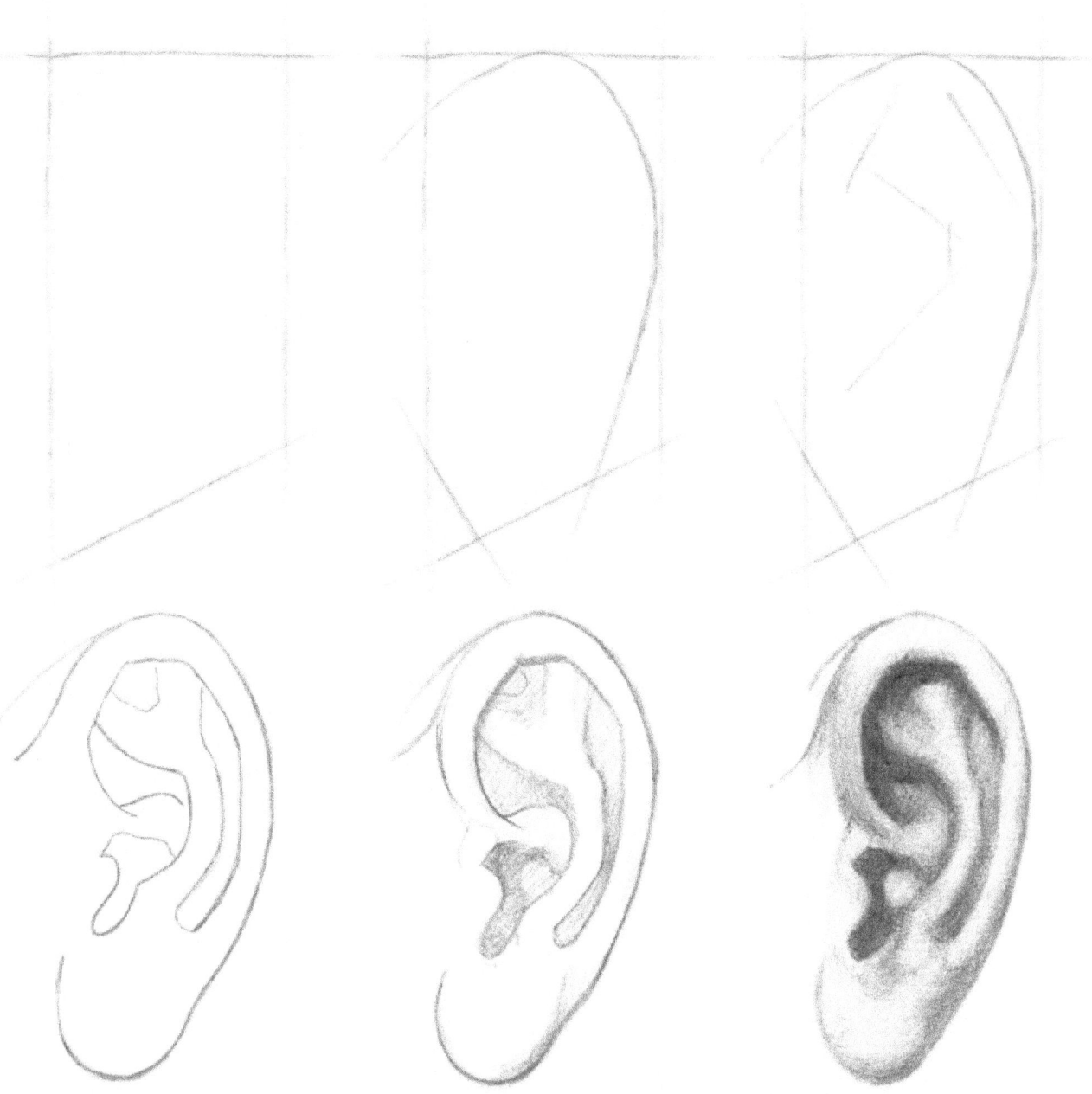

Explain the basic ideas

Step 1: Start by creating the basic shape of the ear. Turn it slightly and note the oval or egg shape. This will give you a plan to build on.
Step 2: Divide the ear into sections with small lines that follow the natural curves and structure. These guidelines help you validate the content.

Download the internal structure

Step 3: Start adding ideas internally. Use guidelines to draw key features in the ear, e.g. Helix (outside edge), .
antihelix (central shell parallel to the helix), .
conch (the cup-shaped part that goes into the ear), .
tragus and antitragus (a small opening near the ear canal).

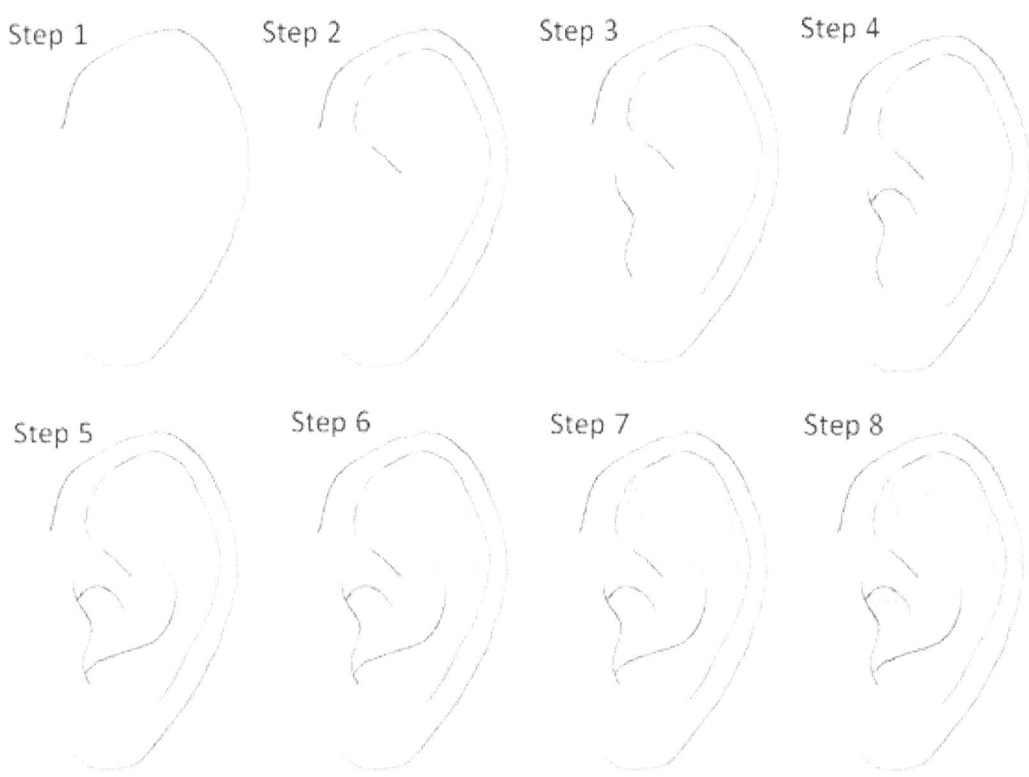

Separate and elaborate

Step 4: Separate and clarify the concepts and move on to your first line. Add more detail to the inner folds and folds, making sure they follow the natural structure of the ear.

Add Shading to create Depth

Step 5: Add shading to give the ears depth and realism. Note the dark areas in the shell, the helix, and the antihelix. Use shadows to contrast the raised and sunken areas of the ears, enhancing the three-dimensional appearance.

This technique helps to capture the intricate shape and texture of the ear in the right amount. This practice of practice can give you the ability to draw from different angles and improve the depth of your images.

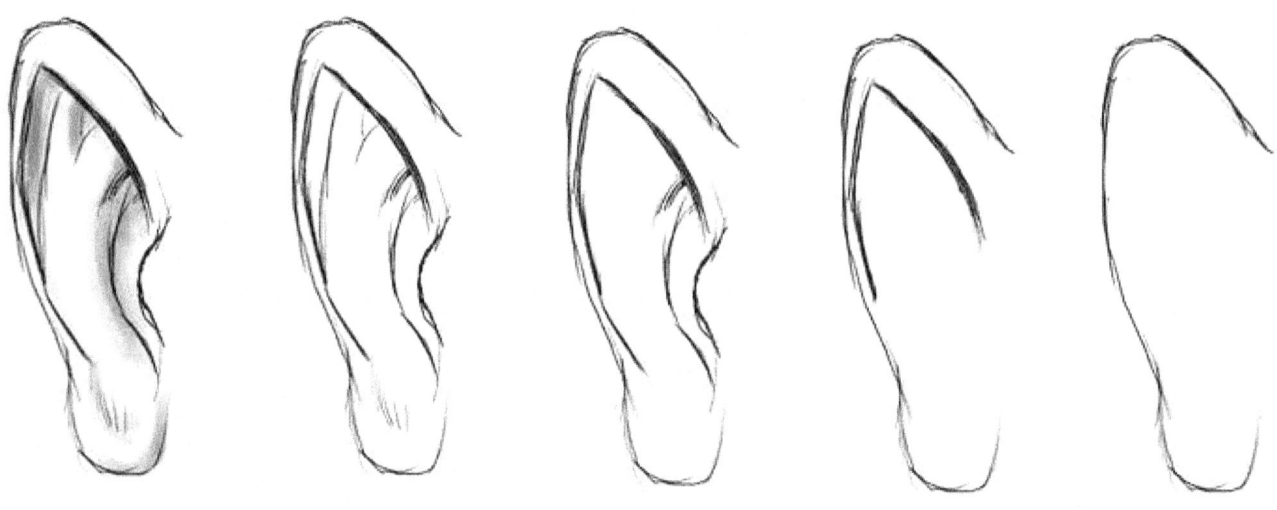

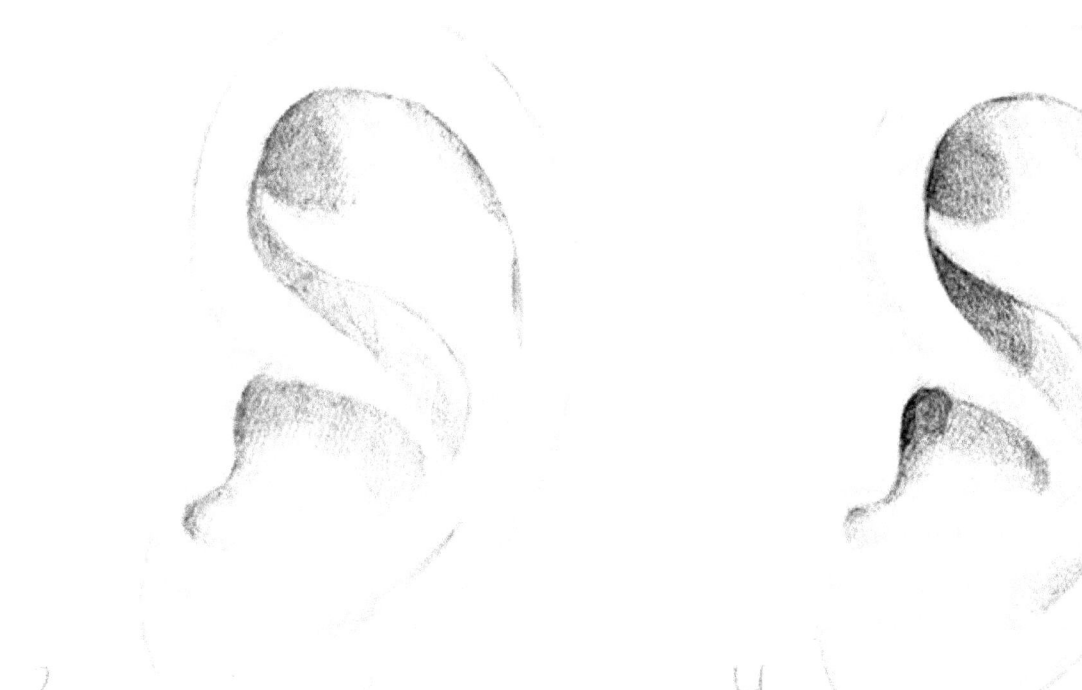

1.

2.

3.

4.

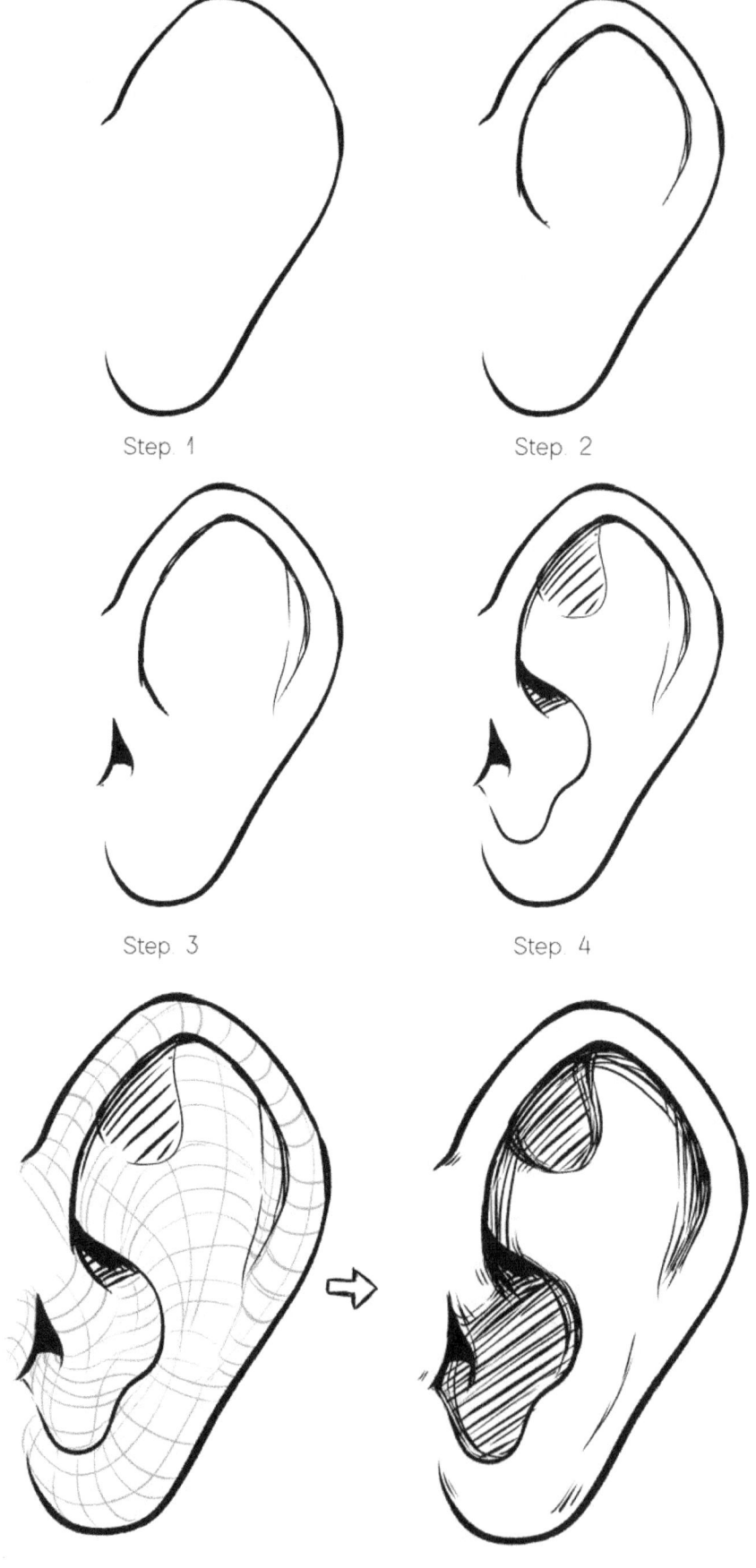

Step. 1

Step. 2

Step. 3

Step. 4

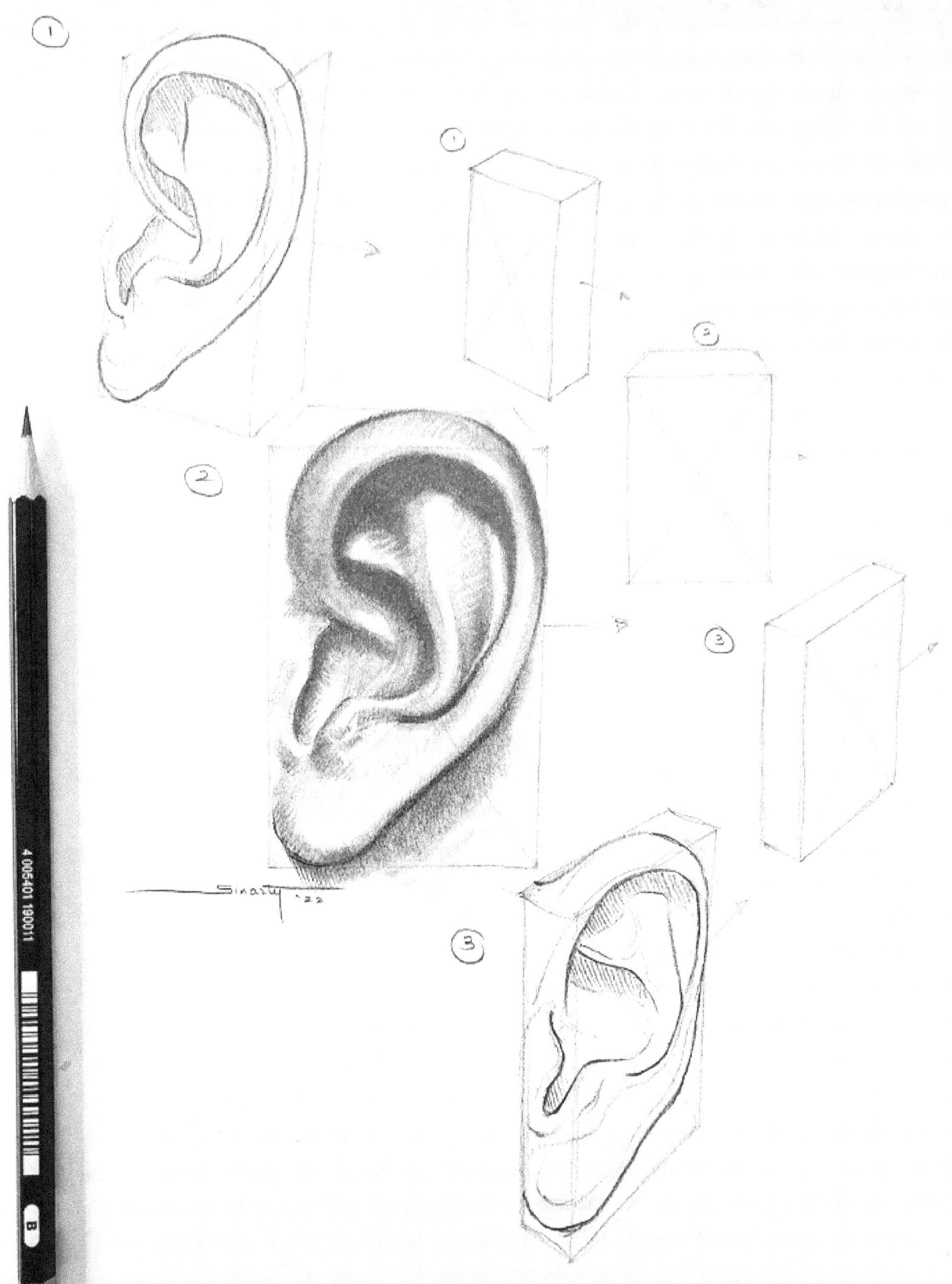

Drawing the human body can seem complex, but breaking it down into simple shapes and proportions makes it much easier. Here's a step-by-step guide to help you get started with basic human anatomy.

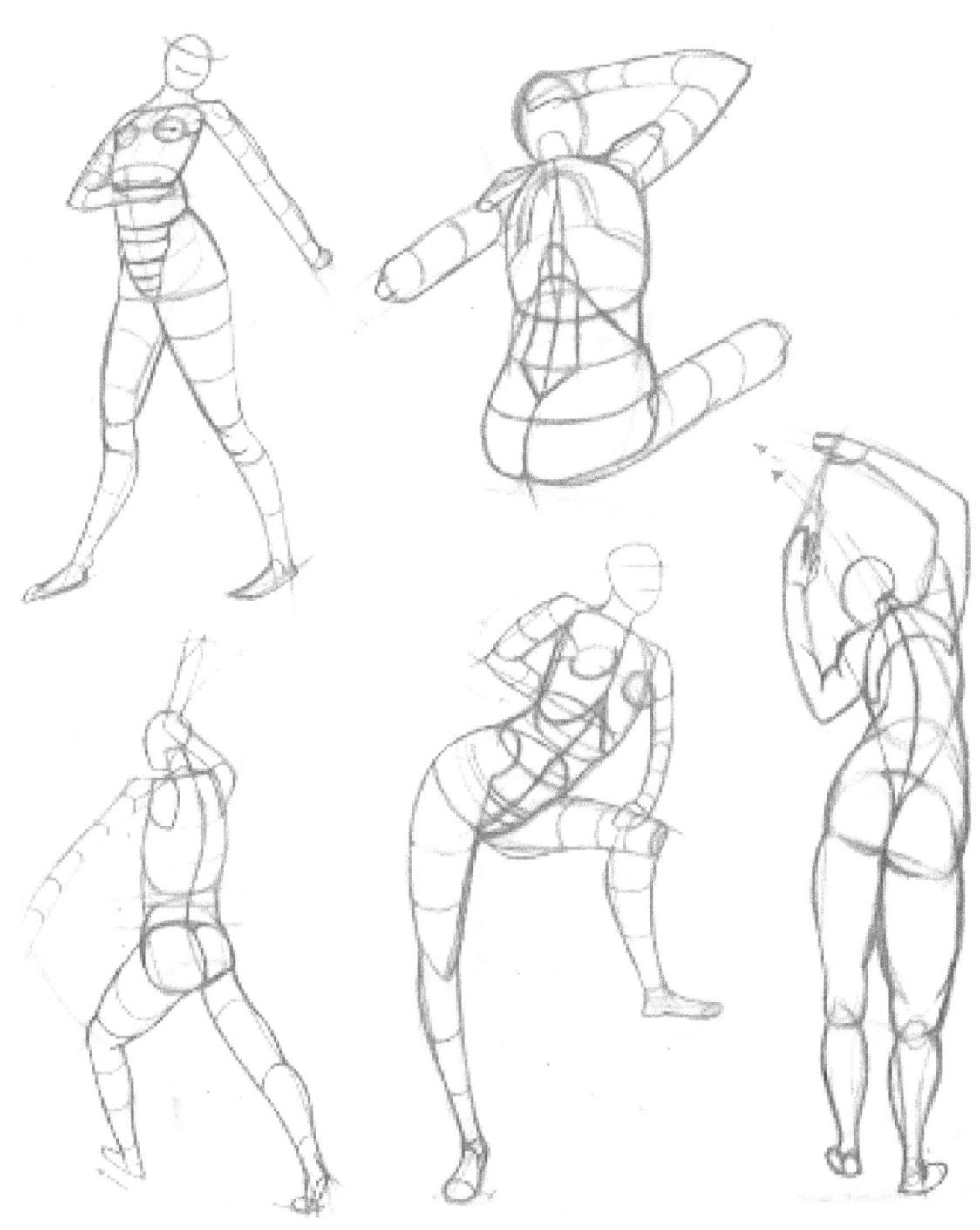

Start with a basic skeleton or tree drawing

Draw lines for the spine to define posture and balance.
Add bands to your shoulders, arms, waist and legs. Simplify this list to mark ideas and donate money.
Add circles or eggs for joints (shoulders, wrists, hips, knees, ankles).

Limb and spinal obstruction

Draw a triangle or triangle for the back, slightly inclined to the position of the body.
To adopt a natural position, turn your ribs in the opposite direction and draw a small oval or box for your pelvis.
Line your ribs and hips together to create a waistline.

Add simple organ shapes

Block the top pieces with a cylinder or rectangle** for the arms and legs.
The upper arm (shoulder to elbow) should be the same length as the wrist (wrist to elbow).
The thighs (thighs to knees) and calves (knees to feet) should also be about the same size.
Remember that the arm and leg joints are slightly curved.

Draw the Head

Draw an oval for the head, slightly smaller than the ribcage.
Place it on top of the spine and align it with the pose. The head should be proportional to the body (usually, the human body is about 7-8 heads tall).

Define Hands and Feet

For the hands, start with a simple shape, like a square or rectangle, to represent the palm, then add small lines for the fingers.
For the feet, draw triangular shapes for the general shape and add smaller shapes to suggest the toes. Keep it simple, as hands and feet can be refined later.

Refine the Body Outline

Now that you have the basic structure, go over the shapes with more defined outlines to form the muscles and contours of the body.
The shoulders should curve slightly, and the waist should narrow. The torso can be a bit wider at the top and taper towards the hips.
Add curves and contours to suggest muscles and the natural flow of the body. Keep in mind where the body bends, such as the elbows, knees, and torso

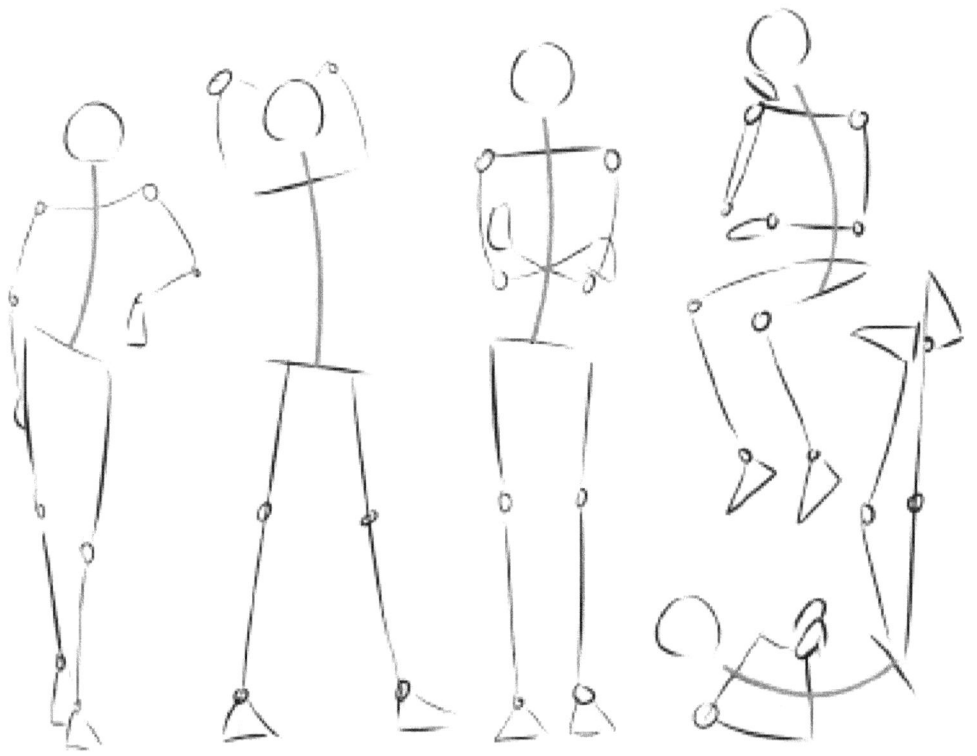

Use ideas

The basic guidelines for dimensions are that the human body is about 7-8 chapters tall:
Ti - 1 ti
Neck and shoulders - about half a head
Coconut thigh - ti
Waist to waist - 1 head
Thighs to knees - 2 heads
From knees to toes - 2 chapters

A quick recap of the main sections:

Arms: shoulder to elbow = elbow to elbow.
Legs: thighs to knees = knees to thighs.
Fuselage: Prow height about 2-3 heads.

Counsel to be used

Draw inspiration from reference photos or look at real people to understand the variation in bodies.
Try different positions to practice the body in different positions. This will help you understand movement and balance.
Practice ideas until they feel natural, and focus on keeping ideas simple and realistic.
Starting from these basic ideas and concepts, you can draw the human body in an organized and manageable way. With it, you can add a lot of detail and sophistication to realistic images.

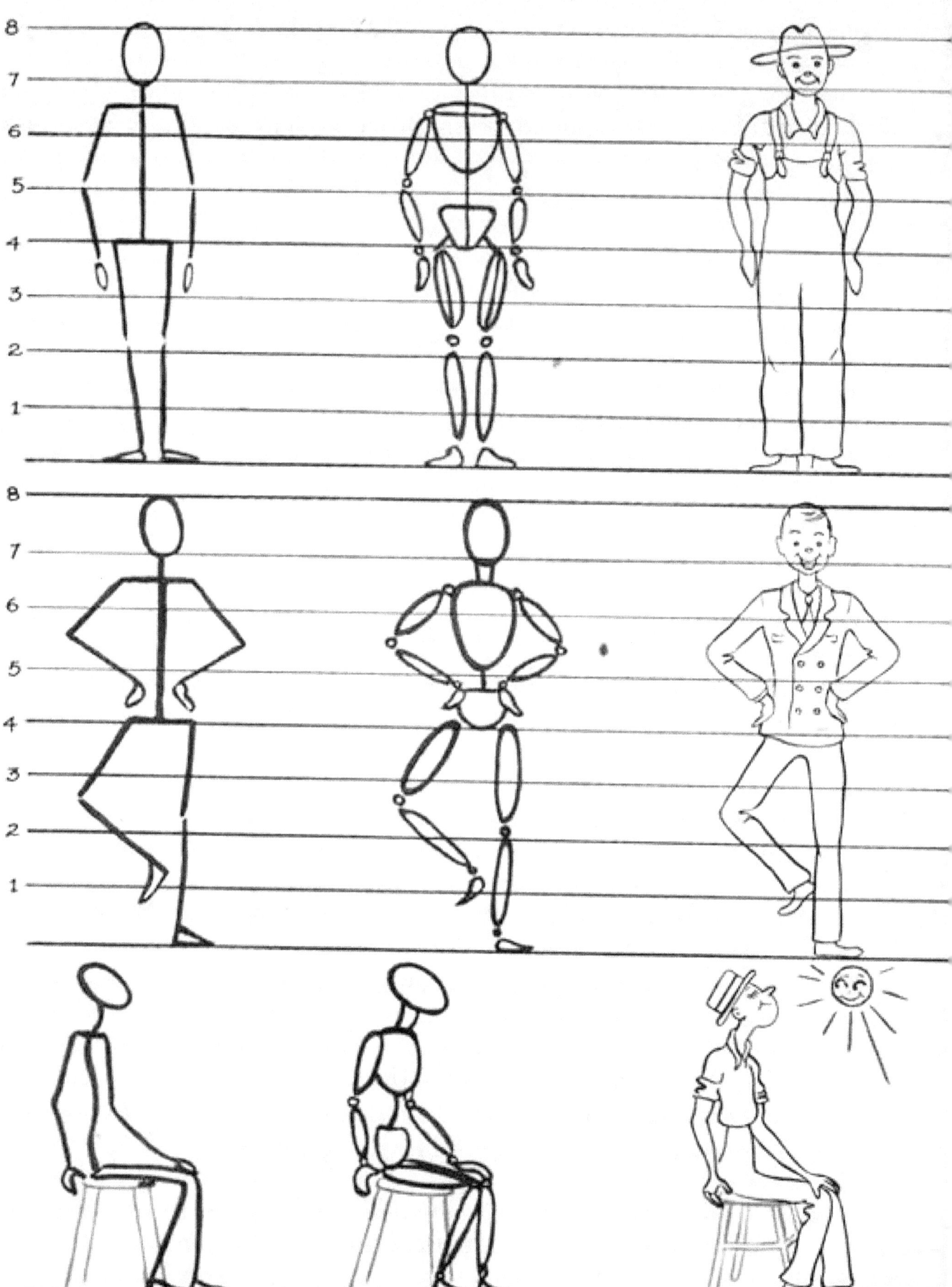

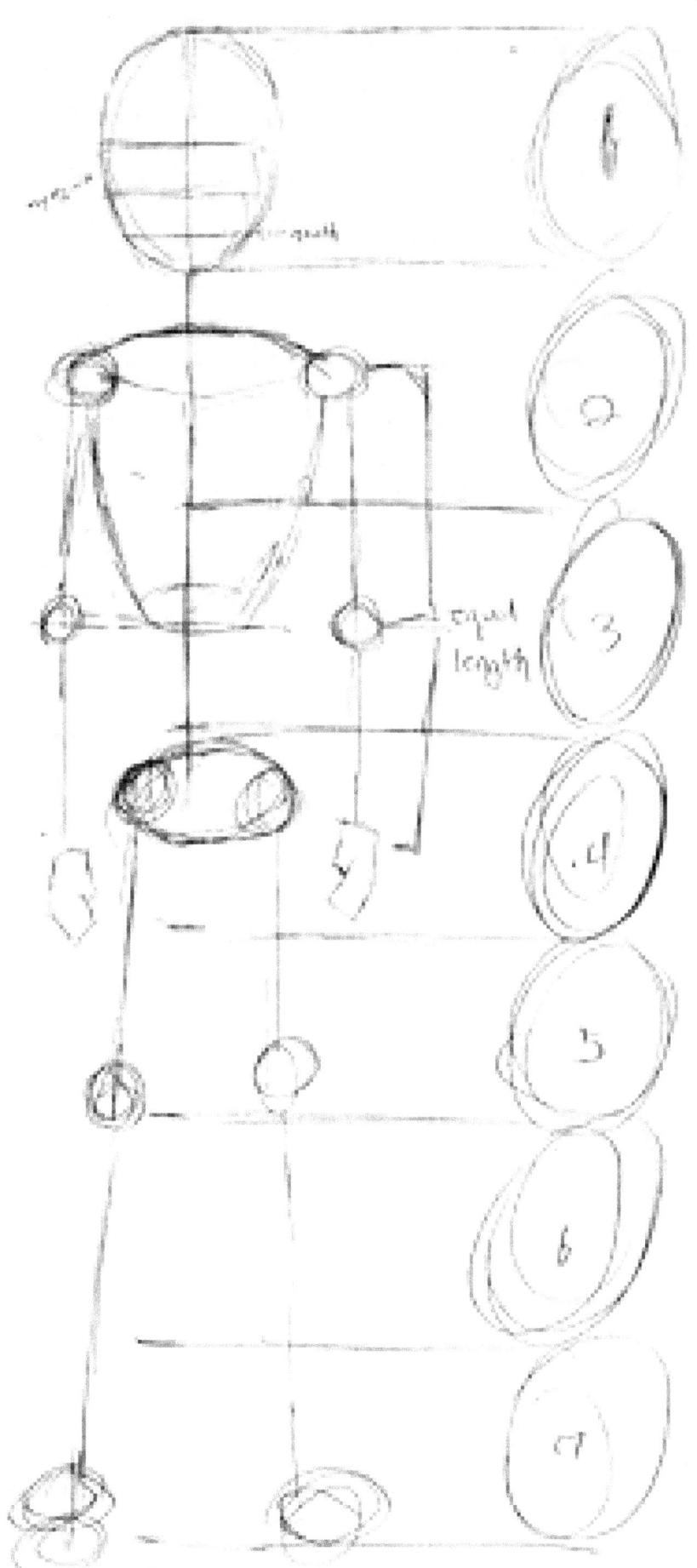

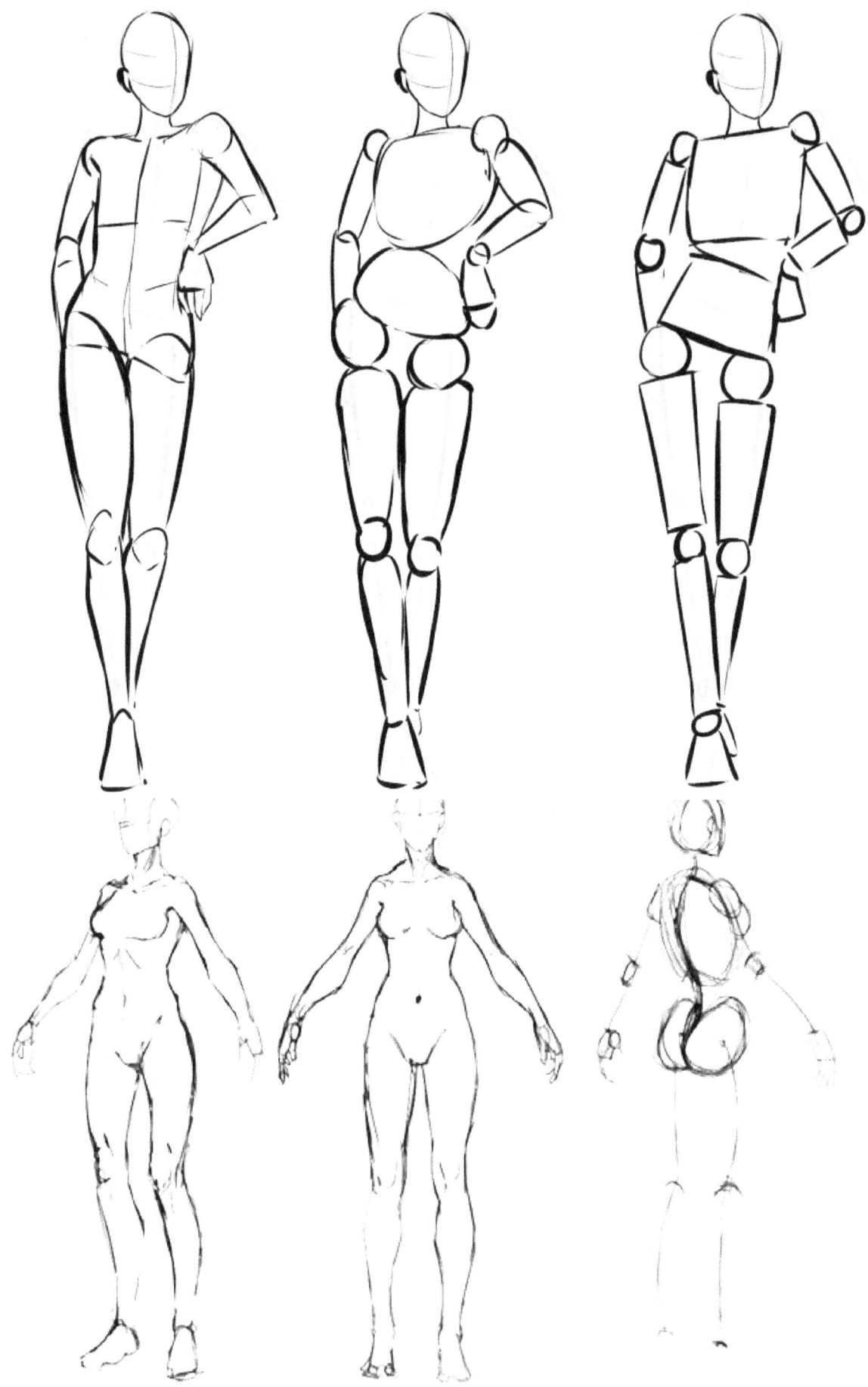

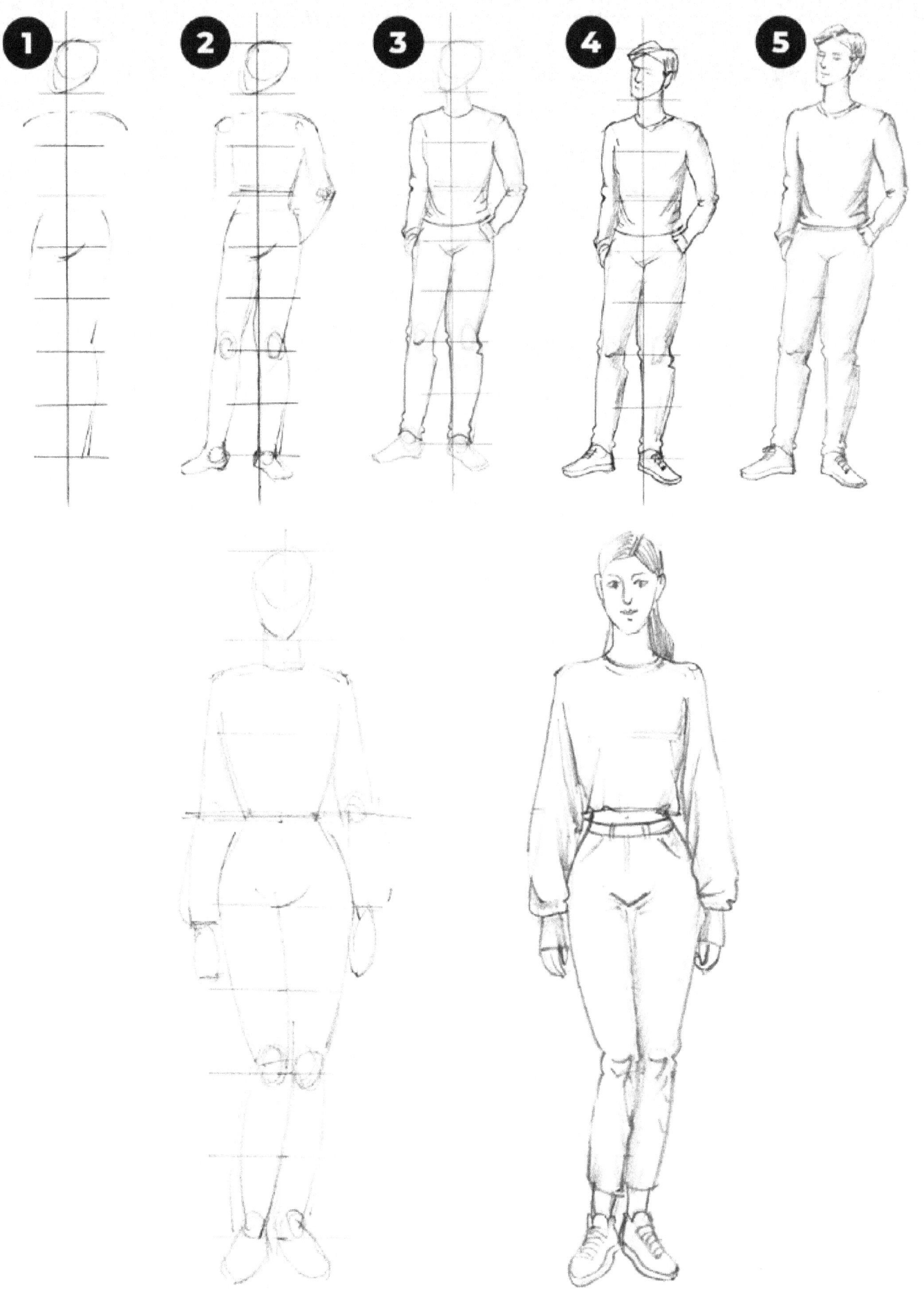

YOUR TURN NOW

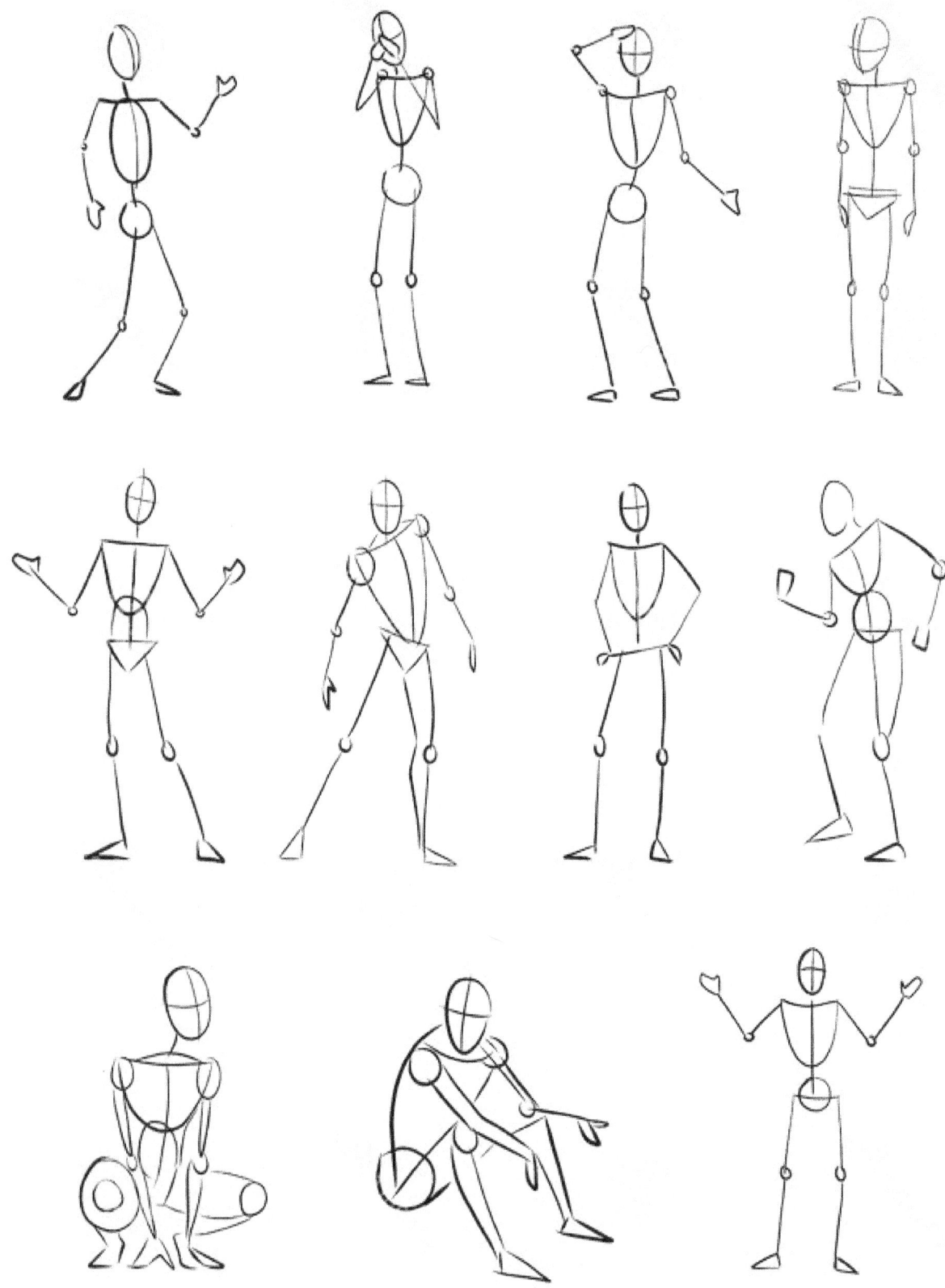

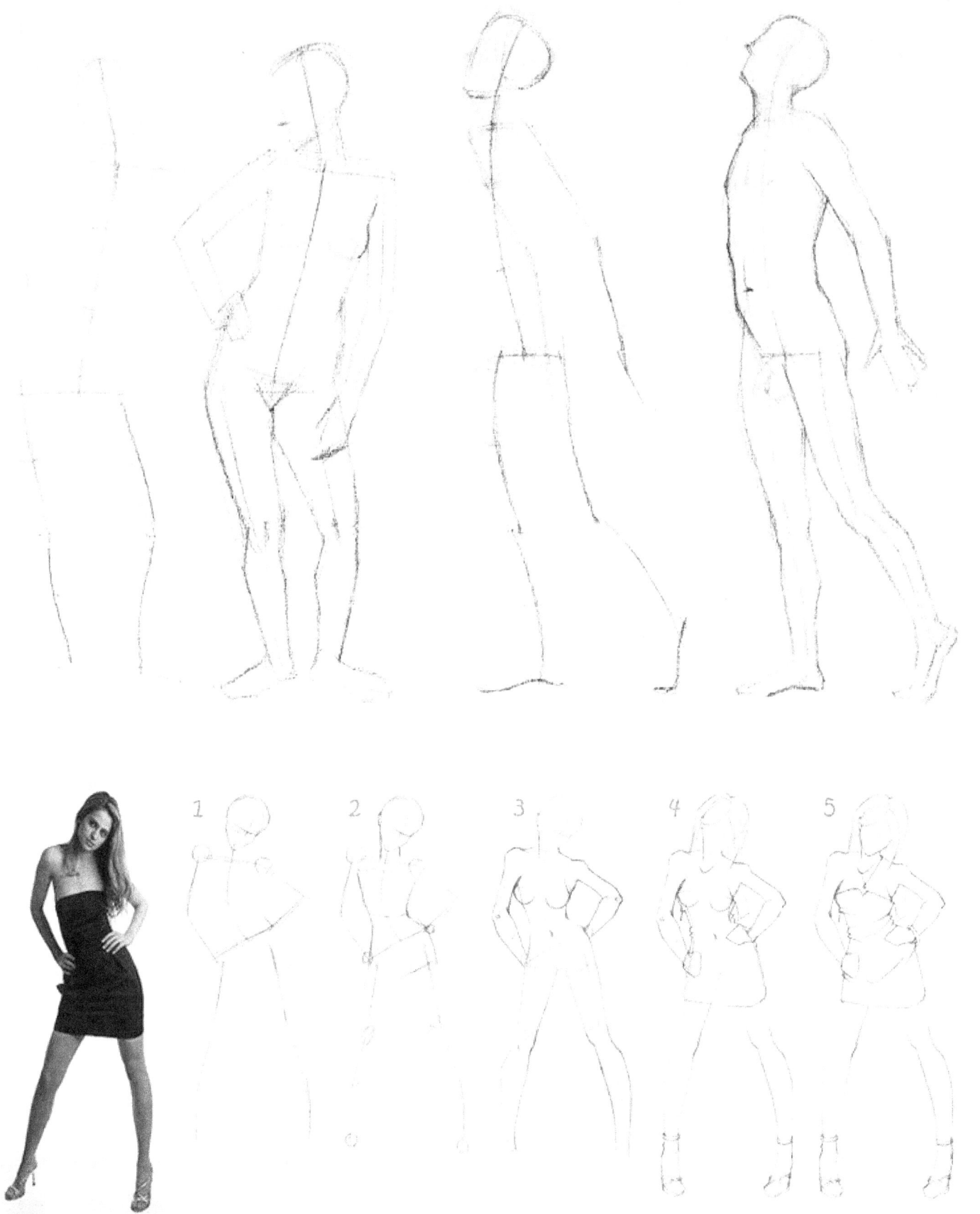

1 2 3 4 5

YOUR TURN NOW

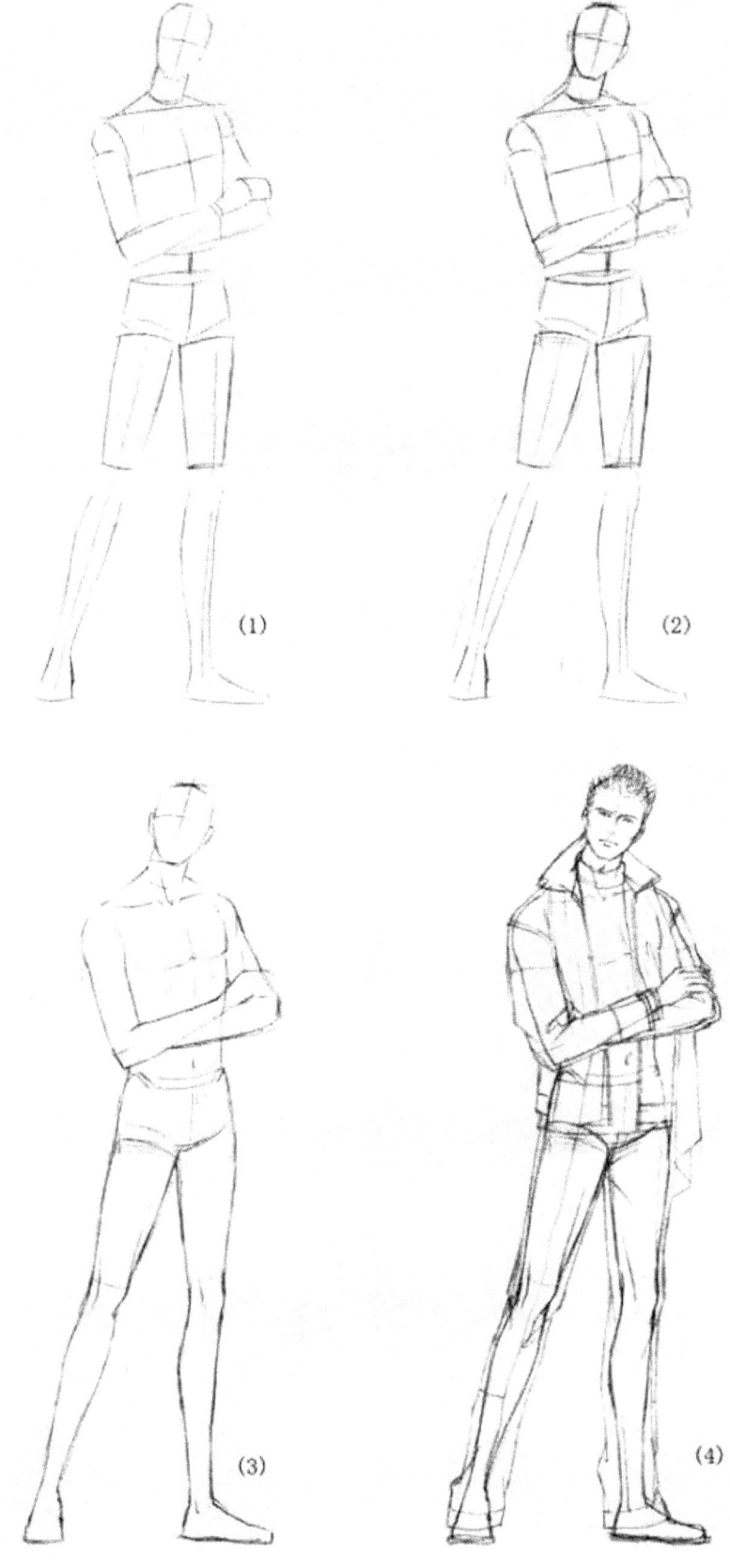

(1)

(2)

(3)

(4)

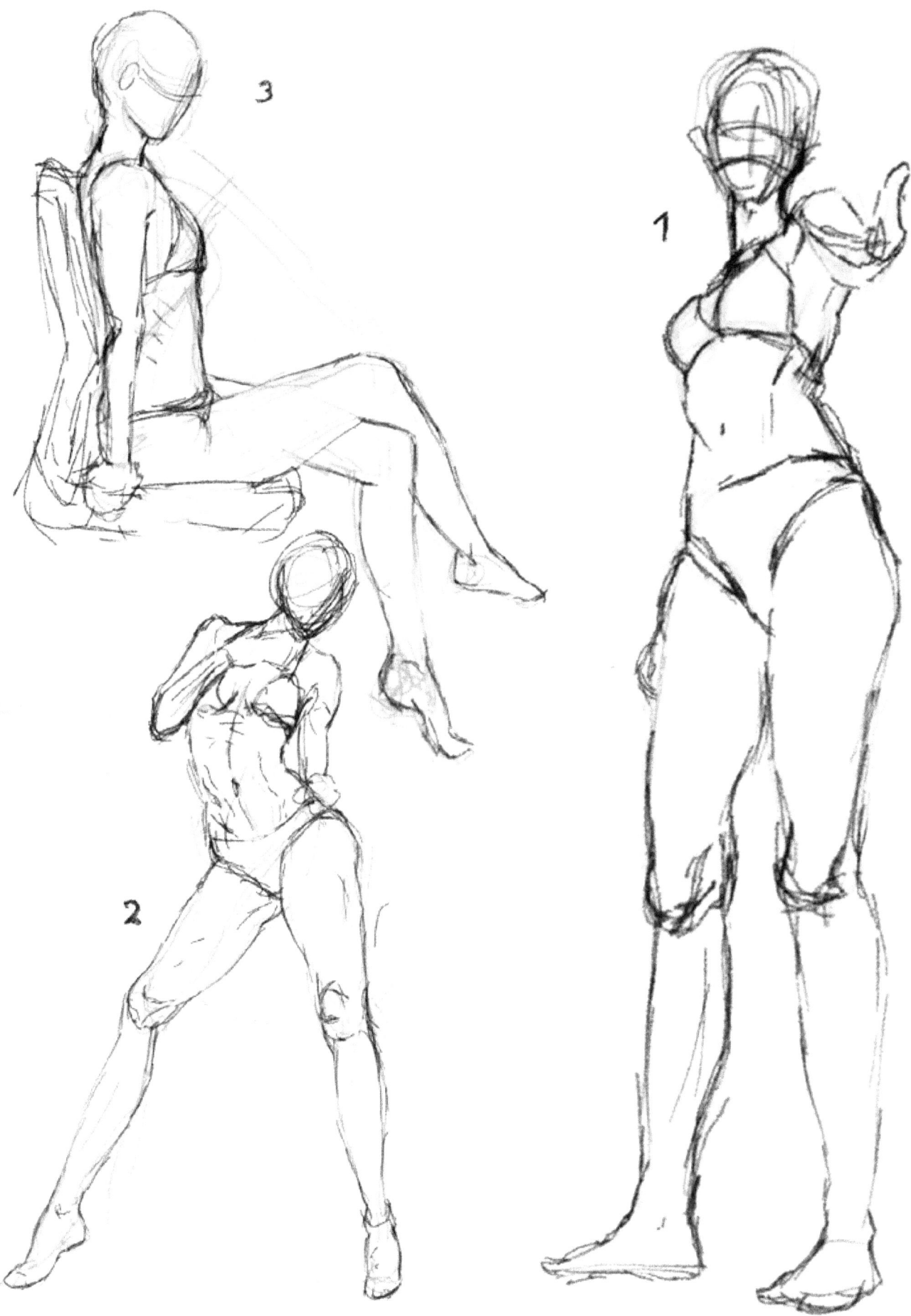

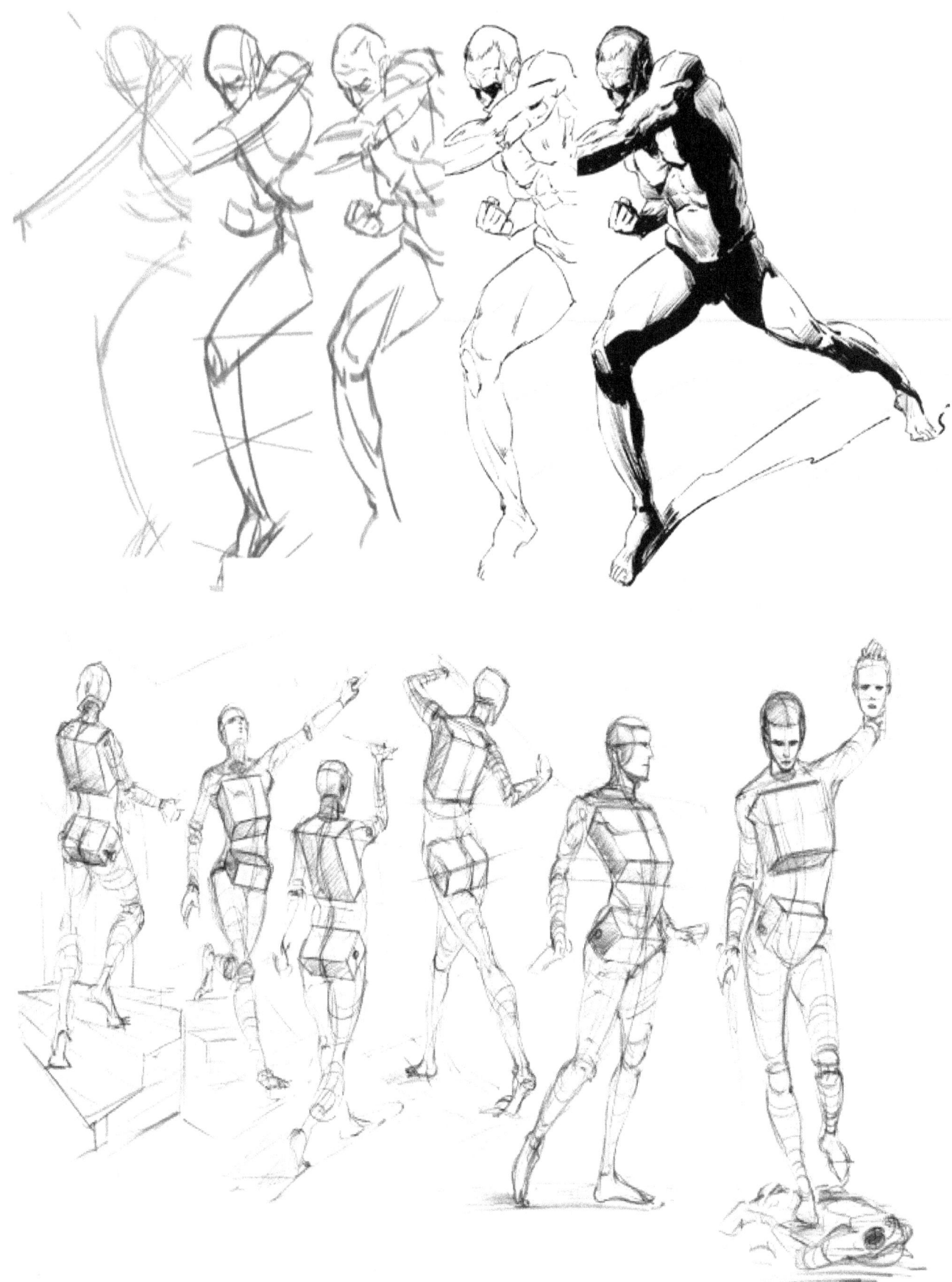

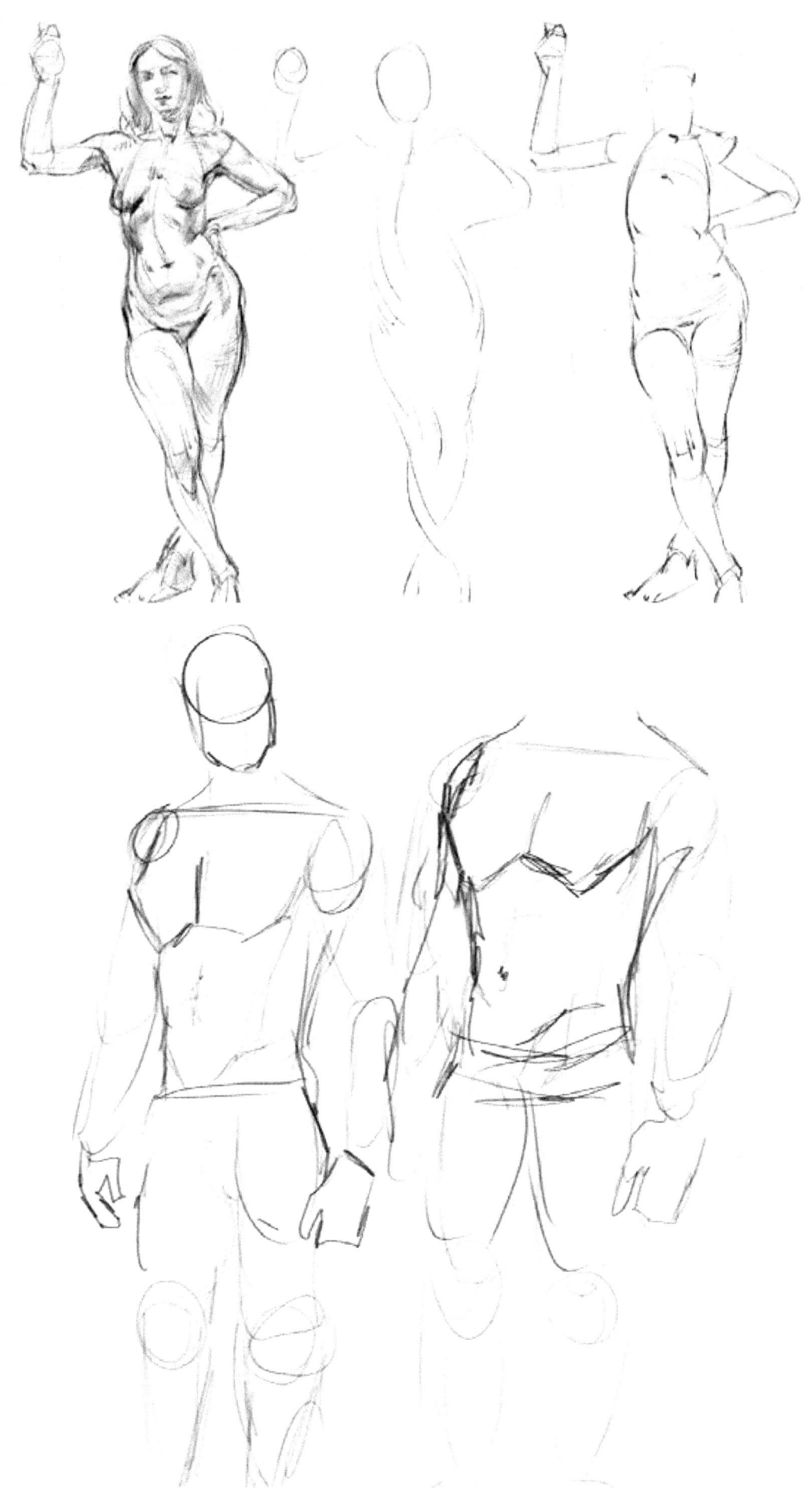

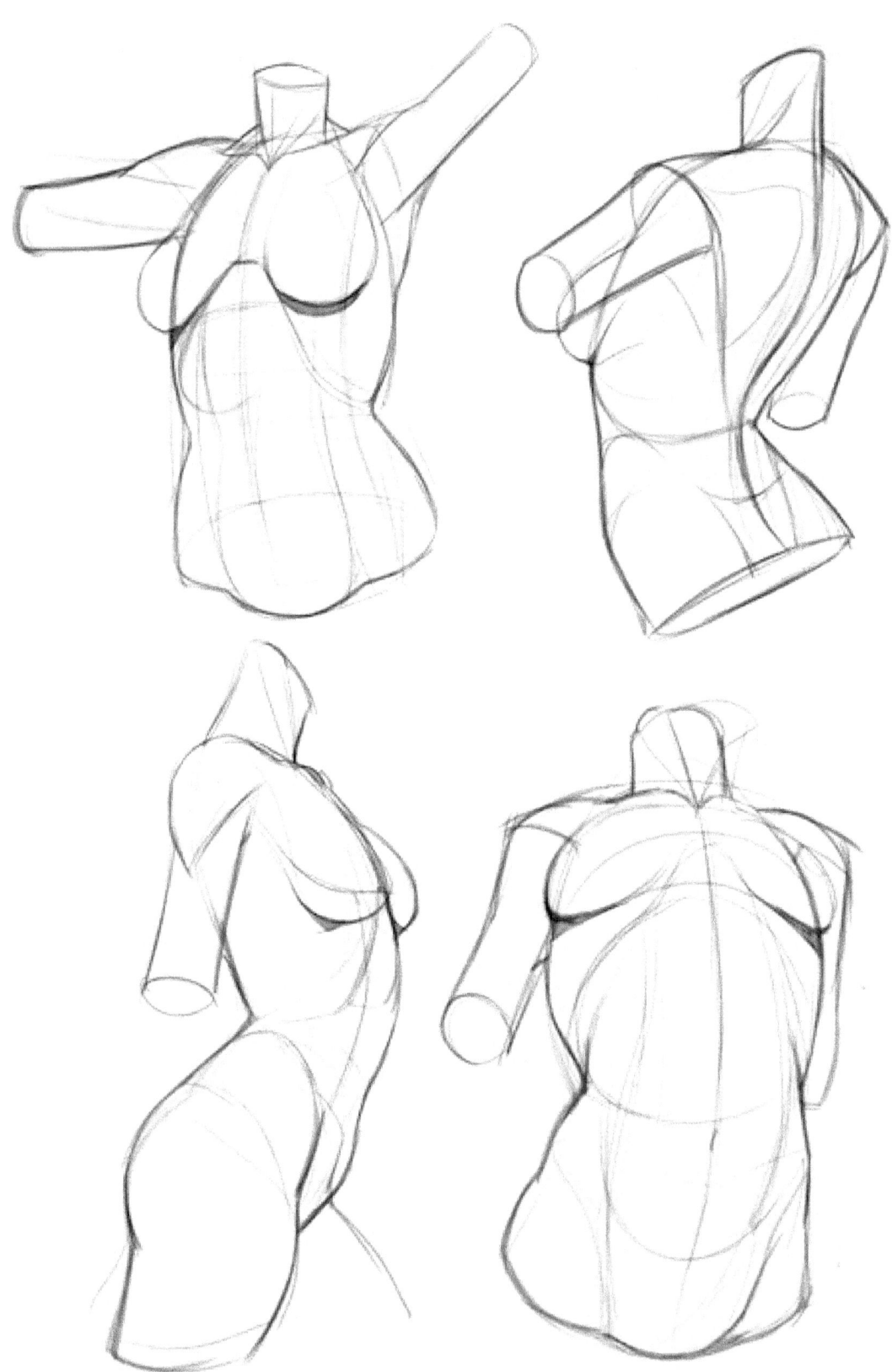